Winter Wellbeing

Winter Wellbeing

SEASONAL SELF-CARE TO NOURISH, SUSTAIN, AND WARM YOUR SOUL

CICO BOOKS
LONDON NEW YORK

Published in 2024 by CICO Books
An imprint of Ryland Peters & Small Ltd

20–21 Jockey's Fields   341 E 116th St
London WC1R 4BW   New York, NY 10029

www.rylandpeters.com

10 9 8 7 6 5 4 3 2 1

A CIP catalog record for this book is available from the Library of Congress and the British Library.

ISBN: 978 1 80065 371 9

Printed in China

In-house editor: Jenny Dye
Designer: Geoff Borin
Art director: Sally Powell
Creative director: Leslie Harrington
Head of production: Patricia Harrington
Publishing manager: Carmel Edmonds

The information in this book is not intended to replace diagnosis of illness or ailments, or healing or medicine. Always consult your doctor or other health professional in the case of illness or for health or dietary advice.

MIX
Paper | Supporting
responsible forestry
FSC® C008047

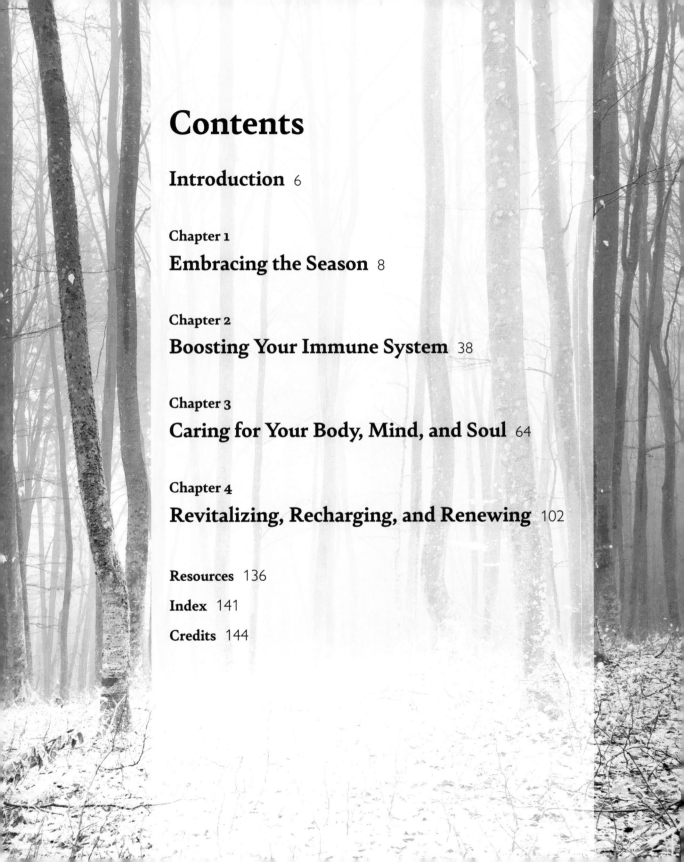

Contents

Introduction

As the days grow shorter and colder, our physical and emotional health can suffer, from fighting off colds and viruses to keeping a positive outlook. This is your guidebook to looking after your health and wellbeing throughout the winter, as well as finding joy and comfort at this time of year.

In the first chapter, discover how to embrace the season, from finding beauty in nature through winter walks to making your living space into a cozy sanctuary. Next, chapter 2 will help you boost your immune health, with recipes for health-giving teas as well as tips for deep and restful sleep. Here you'll also find lots of soothing remedies for winter illnesses, such as a breathing practice for lung issues, healing soups, and teas to combat coughs and colds. Chapter 3 is packed with self-care ideas for your body, mind, and soul, including a self-massage practice, therapeutic bath recipes, and ways to pamper your skin over the harsh winter months. Finally, chapter 4 will help you to reset and thrive, with tips on staying active, a renewing breathing practice, and healthy morning and evening routines.

With self-care practices, nourishing recipes, and ways to appreciate the season, this guide will help you revitalize and recharge your soul, even when it's cold and dark outside.

Chapter 1

Embracing the Season

Winter may be a time of darker days and cold weather, but when we embrace it there are so many small pleasures and moments of comfort to be found. In this chapter, discover how to savor this time of year, from seeing the beauty in nature to taking care of your body and mind through winter walks. You'll also find different ways to celebrate the season, and learn how to use the winter as a perfect time to rest and recuperate.

Winter walks

Sometimes a winter walk is about what is no longer there—birds, flowers, leaves, and sunshine. But with this absence comes more opportunity to pay attention to what *is* there. Empty bird nests are visible, trees take on new forms, revealing their skeletal structure, the north wind shifts from dynamic to ferocious, and of course, snow can descend with a whisper or a clumpy onslaught. Frost paints surfaces with its fractal patterns, and ever-optimistic squirrels and chipmunks grow less timid in hopes of a handout.

Seneca the Younger wrote "All that begins also ends" and winter walks contain beginnings within the endings. Under the slush, frost, and ice, await the first tendrils and promises of spring, and we know that dark days will eventually surrender to the return of light.

Kinhin: mindful walking

When you're walking outside in cold weather, it can feel counterintuitive to slow down and be present. Mindfulness, or any sort of attention or meditation practice, can really help with this. *Kinhin*, or walking meditation, is a practice in Zen Buddhism that involves walking mindfully and slowly. It is more than bringing meditation into the world, it is about experiencing the world and meditation with no separation.

All walking is a meditation of sorts, but kinhin follows a specific path. As meditation teacher Jan Chozen Bays wrote in *How to Train a Wild Elephant*, "Silent walking is a bridge between one side of meditation—silent sitting in pure awareness— and the other side—speaking and moving about."

Kinhin is, of course, about attention, but it is also about slowing down—truly slowing down, which is not as easy as you might think. Here is how to do it:

1 Find a location to walk without distractions. It should be a place where you will not draw attention to yourself, especially if you are outdoors. Make sure the path you have chosen is fairly easy, so that you can focus on just walking, not navigation.

2 Lower your gaze, but do not be inattentive, especially when you are walking outdoors.

3 Become conscious of your breath (but do not control it) as you begin walking slowly—very slowly—and deliberately. Notice the rise and fall of your chest, and the feeling of the air as it enters and leaves your lungs. Perhaps it slows to the point of synchronizing with your steps.

4 Feel the entire motion of your footfall, from heel touching ground to toe rising, as your weight shifts. Then the next step, and the next.

5 Your pace should be slow enough that you can remain aware of each step and breath. Now, move even more slowly...

6 Be aware of your body. As you walk, pay attention to your posture and your body's alignment. Keep your back straight and your shoulders relaxed. All the while, notice the sensations in your feet as they contact the ground and your breath in unison.

FINDING STILLNESS

When practicing this walking meditation, do not swing your arms or put your hands in your pockets. There is a reason why Zen Buddhist monks walk with their hands clasped in front of them in *gassho* (prayer position) or in *shashu* (right hand over left fist)—it helps to create stillness of the body, which offers stillness of the mind.

7 Let go of thoughts. Use the process of walking and breathing to keep you connected to the present moment.

8 Be compassionate and patient with yourself. Your mind will wander, and when it does, gently bring it back to your breath or your body. There is no need to judge yourself or get frustrated. You will find that this practice will allow you to gradually develop the ability to stay in the present moment for longer periods of time.

9 After walking for a while at the slowest pace possible, you can adjust your speed to fit your level of comfort. Zen kinhin usually begins almost impossibly slowly (especially if you are a city dweller who is used to walking fast) and then can pick up to a comfortable, brisk, or even fast pace.

10 There is no set time for kinhin, which is another reason why it is easy adapt to walking outdoors, even in winter. You can practice for as long as you like.

Magical breath

When breathing outdoors during the winter—inhaling cold air and exhaling clouds—we are reminded that our breath is not merely an idea or concept, but physical—made up of gases and vapor.

When it comes to making our breath visible, it is the vapor that is key. Our bodies are composed of almost 70 percent water and the air in our lungs is saturated with water vapor, which is at the same temperature as our bodies—98.6°F (37°C). Cold air does not retain as much moisture as warm air, so when we exhale on a winter's day, the heat of our breath meets the chill air and, for a moment, reaches dew point (the temperature that creates condensation). This forms the droplets of water that create ephemeral, misty clouds.

Seeing our breath makes us more conscious of the many ways that breathing is a spiritual experience—from watching a newborn baby gulp their first lungful of air to holding the hand of a loved one as they exhale their last. It seems apt that the word "spiritual" is derived from the ecclesiastical Latin, *spiritualis*, which means not only "pertaining to spirit" but interestingly "of or pertaining to breath, breathing, wind, or air."

CHI WALKING

A lovely way to pay attention to the breath and "meditate in motion" on winter days is by taking up a practice called chi walking. Start by standing with your feet shoulder width apart and your arms relaxed at your sides. Take a few deep breaths and focus on your body. As you exhale, begin to walk slowly, taking long, conscious, deliberate steps.

As you walk, imagine that you are sending energy (chi) from your feet into the ground, creating an energetic connection and cycle. Visualize chi as breath when it has condensed into clouds, surging and wafting through your body, from your nose as you inhale to the soles of your feet.

Appreciating the outdoors

From the beauty of frost and snow to the stars in a dark night sky and the light of the moon, winter provides so many opportunities for finding wonder in nature. Allow yourself to slow down and appreciate the sights and sounds of the winter season around you.

The wonder of ice

Take a moment to think about ice. Isn't it amazing? A liquid becomes a solid that can return to liquid and the cycle can repeat again and again. Such a nice metaphor for transformation and impermanence.

Ice is the solid state of water, typically formed at or below temperatures of 32°F (0°C). When moisture in the air meets these conditions, ice crystals form and it falls from the sky as snow. Walking in the snow is such a thrill, no matter how many times you do it. Especially new snowfall—the fluff, the crunch, the slog, is a sensory experience like no other. Sound is different after a snowfall, absorbed and muffled, offering up a unique kind of silence—even birds and traffic are hushed. Because snow

WINTER WALKING

If you feel yourself losing your balance when you're walking outdoors in snowy or icy weather, bend your knees and lower your center of gravity. Or try out a pair of walking sticks, ice cleats, or even snowshoes.

is such a good insulator it can make walking outdoors invigorating, letting you know where your edges are (especially if you are dressed for the occasion). The smell is the qualia of crisp and blue. And then there is the light—the morning sun sparkling on the snow and fading into eerie blue on a moonlit night. It is all magic.

"Walking in the snow is such a thrill, no matter how many times you do it."

Speaking the language of snow and ice

The Indigenous peoples of Alaska, Canada, and Siberia have inhabited the vast Arctic regions of North America for generations and are adept at communicating in snowy conditions and landscapes. A stone landmark called an inuksuk is used by Inuit and other Indigenous peoples to guide travelers, warn of danger, assist hunters, or mark places of reverence.

There is a cliché (actually, a myth) that the Indigenous peoples have fifty words for snow. Scholars, beginning with anthropologist Franz Boaz in the 1880s, have deliberated on this, and although it is not exactly the case, the Inuit language and related dialects have myriad words that evoke snow and ice, some poems unto themselves. The Inuit language describes ice with poetic clarity and precision:

- Freshwater ice, for drinking
- The first layer of thin ice formed on puddles in fall
- New ice appearing on the sea or on rock surfaces
- Ice that looks like windows
- Ice that breaks after being tested with a harpoon
- Ice that has cracked because of tide changes and has refrozen
- Slushy ice by the sea

All these words remind us that there are so many levels of perception. Just as we can walk the same path many times and have a new experience or realization each time, so we can look at the same thing—be it snow or ice—and come to it in a whole new way.

THE SOUND OF SNOW

Try listening to ice after a snowstorm—the crackle, the drip, the silence. And if you are snowed in and housebound, there is a simple meditation practice that you can do indoors. Place an ice cube on a dish. Sit still, and in a comfortable position nearby, watch the ice cube melt. Every time your mind strays, return your attention to the process of ice returning to water.

A stargazing walk

In winter the sky is more discernable—this is the gift the trees give between releasing their leaves and budding again. The planets and stars seem closer, more visible. The winter nights are longer, giving us more time to observe the heavenly bodies as they move through the sky. All of these are reasons why winter can be the best time for a stargazing walk.

Winter nights tend to be clearer than summer nights. Cold air is denser than warm air, so it does not hold as much moisture, and less vapor means less haze and fewer clouds. On clear, cold nights, especially if you can find a place free of urban light pollution, it is possible to see about 3,000 stars with the naked eye, even some of the most distant and faintest stars in the night sky. So, while you are walking, look up!

Of all the lights in the sky, no matter the season, the moon is the most captivating. This winter moon has inspired names that feel like poetry: the *Cold Moon* because it occurs during the coldest time of year in the Northern Hemisphere. The *Hunger Moon* because it occurs during a time when animals are hibernating, and plants are scarce. *Cheechakon* is a name given by Indigenous American Algonquins, which means "the moon when the geese return." Yet no matter the label, the winter moon is often seen as a symbol of hope and renewal. It marks the end of winter and start of a new lunar cycle, as spring can be glimpsed just over the horizon.

Full moon tea

Savor and celebrate the light of the full moon with this refreshing herbal brew. Hedgewitches and wise women have been making this delightful concoction for centuries. It is made in the same way as Sun Tea, which is gently heated by the warmth of the sun, but is brewed at night in the light of the moon. Alternatively, put one herbal teabag in a thermos flask, fill the flask with hot water, and take it with you to enjoy on a stargazing walk (see page 20).

1-quart (1-liter) canning jar with lid

cold, pure spring water

4 herbal teabags or 3 heaping tablespoons of dried herbs of your choice

large tea ball or small muslin bag (if using dried herbs)

Fill the jar with the spring water and add the herbal teabags (or the tea ball/muslin bag filled with the dried herbs). Seal the lid on the canning jar and leave it outside or on your windowsill so it can be exposed to the light of the moon. When you awaken in the morning, you will have cold-brewed tea.

HERBS FOR FULL MOON TEA

Here are a few suggestions for herbs and plants to use for your full moon tea, or for traditional tea to enjoy at any time.

Beautiful blue borage

This sweetly blue flower has long been used to decorate cakes and other sweets, but also has a light and pleasant flavor that makes for a lovely, fruity tea. You might want to grow borage in your garden because it attracts pollinators such as bees. Borage tea is very calming and is a marvelous anti-inflammatory.

Delightful dandelion

The gardener's bane should actually be greeted gladly, as these humble yellow weeds are superfoods! They make a hearty and healthy tea, and are excellent as salad greens, so you can take advantage of all the nutrients. If that was not enough, dandelions can also be used to make excellent wine!

Healing hyssop

Both the beautiful purple flowers of hyssop and its leaves have a tangy licorice flavor. This true medicinal can be used from stem to leaf to flower for brewing soothing teas to relieve pain, quiet respiratory complaints, and support your digestion.

Noble nasturtiums

These reseed themselves, so you only need to plant them once and you will have a salad green, a spicy tea, and gorgeous flowers that cheer you up every time you see them. The leaves of the sun-colored flower can be dried and brewed in a tea that is packed with vitamin C and is capable of both healing and preventing colds and flu.

Lovely lavender

While it is nearly universally used as an oil, lotion, and aromatic, it is often forgotten that it makes for a terrific tea. Add bergamot and you will get both an energy boost and a sense of calm. In this case, just breathing in the scent of lavender tea will bring serenity and wellbeing.

Radiant rose

Flavors of rose tea vary depending on the variety and growing conditions, so petals can be both spicy and sweet, but in general darker petals have more flavor. Brewed into a tea and sweetened with honey, rose will attract love into your life and a sense of self-love as well. The scent and energy of rose is very gentle and will raise your vibration and uplift your personal energy.

Vivid violet

This tea might be the most unusual of all, as it has an enchanted color and can be used to brew a lovely blue-green tea that helps with pain relief, insomnia, and coughs. Johnny-jump-ups and their cousin pansy can be used as well. Utterly charming and good for you, too!

Rest and hibernation

Winter has a bad reputation, but despite the boots and the heating bills, it does have positive effects. The longer nights and the fact that our mobility is limited by ice and snow allow us to rest more and sleep for longer. Being stuck indoors and watching snow fall has been described by some as a meditative or contemplative experience. Even without the cardio workout of shoveling, snow brings health benefits that help us to weather the dark days. Exposing the body to cold temperatures (cryotherapy) can raise our levels of norepinephrine, a chemical in the nervous system that may play a role in lessening pain.

In Russian and Scandinavian countries, it is quite common to see babies napping outdoors in their strollers, even when the weather is very cold. Research by Marjo Tourula of the University of Finland found that leaving infants (carefully bundled in warm clothing) outside to sleep in really cold weather not only promotes better sleep, but also increases the length of the nap. The parents she interviewed believed that napping in the fresh air promoted health in their infants, helping them to grow hearty and develop resistance to disease, especially colds. Parents keep an eye on their babies and do not let them get over-chilled, and in Sweden they subscribe to the saying, "There is no bad weather, just bad clothing."

Winter's sleep remedy

Cold weather is a natural sleep aid in many ways. Not only because the nights are longer and darker and our beds somehow cozier, but because cold exposure during the day can improve the quality of our sleep at night, especially as we get older. Scientists from Tohoku Fukushi University monitored those who were exposed to a cold or cool environment—around 55°F (13°C)—for an hour before bedtime and measured their sleep. The results showed that exposure to cold was associated with an increase in slow-wave sleep (our deepest sleep state) and a decrease in wakefulness after falling asleep.

Long winter nights help us sleep in other ways as well. In winter we produce more melatonin (the hormone that helps to regulate sleep–wake cycles). This signals to the body that it is time to conserve energy, and so promotes sleep. If cold weather can improve our sleep, then walking in winter can improve it even more. According to psychologists from Brandeis University, walking can have a marked effect on how long and well we sleep. When they focused on people like those with insomnia, residents of nursing homes, those with depression, cancer, and Alzheimer's disease, and women transitioning through menopause, they found a direct correlation between walking and improved sleep efficiency. Participants showed reduced nighttime wakefulness and next-day fatigue, as well as a decrease in depressive symptoms. A more general study found that people who walked for 30 minutes in cold weather, five days a week for a month had improved sleep quality compared to those who did not. So, even on the coldest days, bundle up, put on sturdy boots, and go for a walk—especially if you are having trouble sleeping.

SAVORING THE COLD

So often we are in a hurry to get out of the cold, but when you are able, take a moment to pause and be *with* the cold. Try to give the sensation as much attention and appreciation as you would summer sunlight on your skin or a fragrant spring breeze. There is a benefit—an energetic stillness—in being with cold that is so easy to miss. Allow yourself to savor it.

Natural light and darkness

Daylight matters a lot—almost as much as sleep. We can't all live in Los Angeles or Athens, and those of us in areas that receive less sunlight over the year—such as London, Seattle, or Juneau, Alaska—are prone to seasonal affective disorder (SAD), which disturbs our physical and mental health. Dr. Norman Rosenthal was the first to give a name to this form of depression that so many of us experience in winter, brought on by fluctuations in the release of serotonin by the brain. We now know that doing things that will stimulate our brains to produce more melatonin and skin to produce more vitamin D will help with SAD, and we can find other ways to lighten up, too.

Recent studies and patient care at institutions such as the Center for Light Treatment and Biological Rhythms at Columbia University's Medical Center suggest that light therapy may contribute to the treatment of depression, bipolar disorder, Alzheimer's disease, and particularly SAD. Researchers don't yet know exactly how light works, but they believe that exposure to bright, full-spectrum artificial light during the day resets the circadian clock. This helps people with SAD recalibrate their internal clocks, especially in the winter, when mornings are dark and our natural rhythms shift.

One thing we can do about this is to pay more considered attention to our working and living environments. Increasingly, architects are seeking to maximize opportunities for natural light and darkness in the design of buildings, whether homes, hospitals, or offices. Remember that until the start of the twentieth century our primary source of light was sunlight. Artificial light is a new phenomenon in our biological history.

The nineteenth-century Danish physician Niels Ryberg Finsen was one of the first modern scientists to name and promote light therapy as a medical treatment, and was awarded the Nobel Prize in Medicine in 1903. Since then, there have been many proponents of this basic healing method. Light box therapy is a good option if your lifestyle or job prevents you from connecting to regular day/night rhythms. Most light boxes employ a standard wavelength toward the red end of the color spectrum, usually at an intensity of approximately 10,000 lux, which replicates full daylight but not necessarily direct sun. Opinions as to when and how long to use them vary, so consult a physician or expert before undertaking the treatment.

TAKE A SUN BATH

During the darker winter months, the lack of natural sunlight affects our sleep patterns and overall energy levels, which can lead to depression, sleepless fatigue, decreased motivation, and changes in appetite or sleep patterns. So, whenever you have access to natural light—even through a window— take a sun bath, ideally exposing your uncovered skin to the healing rays.

Balancing your circadian rhythm

Human beings are creatures of rhythm—from our heartbeats to the pace of our breaths to our sleep cycles—and we should be sleeping when it's dark and waking to the light. These repeating patterns are the ticking of our circadian clock (from the Latin *circa*, meaning about, and *dies*, day). Light is the primary and strongest environmental time cue that calibrates the body's internal clock to pretty much a twenty-four-hour cycle. When the days are shorter in winter and we spend more time indoors, it can be difficult to get enough sunlight to support our bodies' natural rhythms. When our circadian rhythm is out of kilter, so are we, and it's like walking around with permanent jet lag.

To optimize our levels of melatonin, the hormone our brain produces at night and that regulates this body clock, we need to be awake when it's light and asleep when it's dark. Exposure to light before bedtime may reduce our sleep quality by suppressing the production of melatonin. This can be a problem particularly in the winter, when we spend more time around artificial lights and on our screens during the dark evenings.

Recent research has found that preschool-age children exposed to too much light at bedtime showed an 88 percent reduction in the production of melatonin (the sleep-promoting hormone), because the structure of their young eyes may make them more vulnerable to the impact of bright light. And numerous studies have shown that looking at computers, smartphones, and even televisions an hour or so before bed can be disruptive for people of all ages, interfering with our circadian rhythms and causing us to postpone falling asleep naturally, making it more difficult to get up the next morning. The best way to avoid this is to turn off devices and as many lights as you can in the evening, or at least dim the brightness and blue tones on screens.

Staying as close as possible to the natural cycles of darkness and light—which usually means going to bed around 10 p.m. and getting up near sunrise—also helps to keep our circadian rhythms balanced and can help to diminish insomnia. As well as during the coldest season, this is especially important as we get older, since it's been shown that aging results in a significant reduction in daylight sensitivity in the part of the brain that controls circadian rhythms.

Here are some more things you can do to help yourself sleep better and live with as little artificial light as possible during winter.

• Eat at regular times, and not within three hours of bedtime.

• When you wake up in the morning, open the curtains, but wait as long as you can before turning on lights or looking at screens.

• Get a good dose of sunlight when you can during the short winter days— see page 27.

• Limit your computer and smartphone time as much as your job or lifestyle permits, and take advantage of timers and orange screen settings to filter the artificial blue light.

• When you walk into a room, pause and don't automatically turn on the light— think about whether you really need it.

• Instead of spending your leisure time looking into lights (watching television, playing video games, or surfing the net), engage in activities where the light is more passive, such as reading, playing board games, cooking or baking, or having a conversation. Keep electronic devices out of your bedroom if possible.

• Block light that seeps into the room where you sleep. Use heavy shades or lots of potted plants (bonuses: green during the day, and cleaner air) to keep the streetlights out.

Celebrating the season

Finding moments of celebration allows you not just to survive but also thrive during the darkest time of the year. Decorating for winter and creating a cozy, comforting haven are excellent ways of finding joy in this season. This section also includes a recipe for hot mulled cider that's perfect for any winter celebration or holiday.

Creating a winter shrine

One way of appreciating the winter season is to decorate a small space or "shrine" in your home—such as a shelf, a mantelpiece, or a table—with gifts from nature. You could also add any objects that are meaningful to you or remind you of winter including beloved objects, candles, foliage and berries, or crystals. Create your shrine any time during the winter, to welcome in the season as the dark nights draw in, or to celebrate the Winter Solstice, the shortest day of the year, which is on December 21 in the northern hemisphere.

When you're deciding how to decorate your winter shrine, consider what speaks to you. Think of how a frozen lake glistens with many colors and the mystery that lies beneath the surface, both of which could be represented by an iridescent and glittery chunk of labradorite crystal for your altar. As you take a walk in the darkening days, you might collect a birch branch covered with delicate lichen, a fallen leaf, which is a perfect dried emblem of the changing of the season, or one tiny acorn, tucked in the roots of an old oak tree, which you can place on your altar as a symbol of all potentiality.

Why not also try your hand at art? Paint on your altar a triptych—the hoary sky, palest sun struggling to shine, a low-hung harvest moon, all beautiful blues with a sapphire night sky and silver stars.

Thinking about the heavens above and the firmament in which hang the stars, moon, sun, and all the planets, you might be struck by a sense of the sacred. It is so special to be alive on this planet; maybe an accident and most definitely a miracle. As you think about it, perhaps you can almost feel the swing of Earth on its axis as it spins around the sun, and now more than ever, feel so very alive.

Hot mulled cider

Perfect for any long winter evening or festive celebration, this warming brew that will not only create conviviality but also imbue your home with a heaven-sent fragrance.

1 gallon (4.5 liters) apple cider

large stockpot

peel of half an orange, cut into pieces. Slice the second half, to garnish

1 heaping teaspoon ginger root, diced

2 star anise pods

3 cinnamon sticks, cut in half, plus extra cinnamon sticks, to garnish

1 tablespoon whole cloves

muslin bag and string to tie

Pour the cider into the pot and place on a low heat. Put the orange peel and the spices into the muslin bag and tie with a string. Now add the spice bundle into the pot and let simmer to a slow boil. Once the brew has reached a rolling boil, turn off the heat and serve delightful and delicious mugs full of magic. Garnish each mug with an orange slice and a cinnamon stick.

Creating a cozy sanctuary

It feels natural to want to hibernate during the colder and darker season, and there's something very comforting about updating your home with the arrival of winter and bringing nature in as it changes outside. In Scandinavia, where the winters are longer and darker, people live with the seasons and decorate their homes accordingly. They get more settled in their homes, because they know they are going to spend a lot of time there.

Taking inspiration from Scandinavian style and seasonal living, try these ways of creating a cozy and welcoming sanctuary to come home to when it's cold and dark outside.

Simple seasonal style

Updating your home for the winter doesn't mean that you have to fill it with extra furnishings or decorations. Many Nordic homes have a feeling of comfort without being overly ornate or cluttered, and incorporate just the right amount of furniture and décor. To use a popularized Swedish word, they are *lagom*, meaning they have just the right amount of stuff—not too much, not too little. Use these pointers to create a relaxing and calm environment for the winter inspired by Nordic style.

• Focus on clean lines and simple, light-colored furniture.

• Remove and store away clutter.

• Think about sustainability—save up for a good piece of furniture rather than getting a mass-produced piece that might not last as long. Shopping vintage and going to thrift stores is one way to give a longer life to furniture.

• Incorporate natural materials and bring the outside in. Collect shells, smooth rocks, branches, and pinecones as they will bring back memories from windswept beaches and peaceful forests.

• Think about home accessories that can create that *hygge* feeling of warmth, simplicity, and coziness. This could be anything that evokes a cozy atmosphere and makes an ordinary moment more special, such as a warm woollen blanket or lighting a candle as you eat your breakfast in the winter.

Bringing the outdoors in

Using nature as a feature in decorating is a key element in Nordic homes, so try these simple ways of bringing seasonal foliage and flowers into your home.

• **Pine decorations**: To make some simple decorations, pop branches of pine in a rustic jar as a mini festive tree. Places selling Christmas trees usually remove the bottom branches of the trees and will normally give the offcuts to you for free. Add some eucalyptus for a more spicy scent. You could also tie several pine branches together with some sturdy string, add a red ribbon, and hang them on the door for an alternative to a wreath.

• **Seasonal flowers**: Buy and plant traditional winter bulbs in pots in early to mid-winter, so that by the time the darkest season rolls around they are out in bloom and make your house smell lovely. You could use hyacinths, amaryllis, or paperwhites. Once in bloom, water the amaryllis and hyacinth sparsely and keep them somewhere cool at night to prolong the flowering. You can keep the amaryllis as a house plant all year round; stop watering and feeding for about eight weeks in fall, and then repot it for another Christmas. Once the hyacinths have bloomed, cut the flower stalks off, keep the bulbs somewhere dry, and then plant them out in a flower bed in spring. Paperwhites, from the Narcissus family, are incredibly easy to grow. Add a layer of small stones to a shallow nondraining bowl. On top, layer the bulbs pointy side up and tightly together, add another layer of stones or compost, and then add water.

Festive stars and lights

In winter when daylight hours are limited, Scandinavians make sure to stock up on candles, tealights and votives. They illuminate dark corners and windows with lamps, either hanging or free standing, and place large lanterns with a candle outside the front door.

• **Window decorations:** Placing a traditional electric seven-arm advent light in a window is one way to create that warm and cozy, or as the Swedes would say *mysig*, atmosphere. Seeing the lights in the window can also bring cheer to passersby. The Nordics traditionally hang star decorations in their windows, perhaps because they feel close to the stars during the long winter nights. A string of fairy lights or a hanging star made from paper, straw, or metal with a light in it would brighten up an otherwise dark window.

• **Winter candles:** To create some beautifully simple candles to brighten up your home, take some small offcuts of pine. Place them on the outside of an empty glass jar and attach them with some rustic twine or a red or white ribbon. Place a tealight in the jar.

Chapter 2

Boosting Your Immune System

As the days grow shorter and colder, it's more important than ever to look after our health so that we can fight off colds and viruses. Here you'll find simple ways to boost your physical wellbeing and avoid falling prey to illness in the first place, as well as soothing natural cures and remedies for seasonal ailments.

Looking after your immune health

This section includes ways to help you to strengthen your immune health so that you can enjoy and make the most of the winter season. Try a breathing exercise that will support your immune system, find tips for getting a peaceful night's rest, and discover recipes for teas packed with immune-boosting ingredients.

Breathing practice for immunity

During the coldest months, try building this simple breathing practice into your daily routine. By reducing stress, it helps to keep the thyroid in balance and support your immune health. The thyroid is a beautiful, butterfly-shaped gland in the base of the throat and, despite its delicate appearance, it is a powerfully important piece of the puzzle that is you. Part of the endocrine system, it produces hormones that regulate breathing, heart rate, metabolism, muscle strength, body temperature, menstrual cycles, mood, brain development, digestion, and bone maintenance. The immune system has a big part to play in every aspect of health, of course, and is closely connected to the thyroid remaining in balance, neither underactive (hypothyroidism) nor overactive (hyperthyroidism). So the thyroid is the perfect place to begin to chart a course of healing. A weak immune system cannot do its detective work to expose the pathogens (disease-causing agents) hiding among the healthy tissues of the body, which affects the functioning of the thyroid and may cause the imbalance that we notice as symptoms of illness. We can address this by restoring some clarity and harmony to our central nervous system (CNS) and soothing the adrenal glands. The CNS and adrenal glands are strongly influenced by the thyroid and the immune system, and are very susceptible to stress. This breathing practice focuses on creating a more harmonious environment and keeping our stress responses in check.

Bee breath

This breath is wonderful for your mood as it balances levels of serotonin, "the happy hormone," in your brain. It relieves stress and sends a healing vibration through the vocal chords and chest.

In a comfortable standing position, or seated either in a chair or on the floor, place one hand on your heart and one hand on your belly. Inhale and as you exhale make a deep humming sound like a bee. Hum from the chest and belly more than from the lips. Let the "breath buzz" fade out naturally. Do not strain for the sound to last, rather let it softly and naturally fade in the way a buzz from a bee fades as it flies farther away from you.

Warming winter tea

This soothing tonic provides bioflavonoids and vitamin C in an organic, natural way so all the nutrients are easily available for absorption. The amounts of ingredients are given in parts, so you can make a big batch of tea for the whole family. Vitamin C plays an important role in supporting the body's immune system, so serve this regularly as a preventative during the cold and flu season.

2 parts lemongrass

3 parts hibiscus

4 parts rose hips

1 part chopped cinnamon sticks

4 cups (960ml) hot water

honey

Blend the herbs using a mortar and pestle. Place in a teapot with the hot water. Steep for 5 minutes in your teapot, then strain and serve sweetened with honey to taste. If you make ahead, you should keep the mixed herbs in an airtight container.

Rosehip and hibiscus tea

Get cozy with this health-giving drink which is ideal for chilly days. The rosehips in this tea contain 50 percent more immune-boosting Vitamin C than oranges. One tablespoon provides more than the recommended daily adult allowance of 90 mg for men and 75mg for women.

1oz (28g) dried rosehips

1oz (28g) dried hibiscus

2oz (56g) dried mint

1 tablespoon dried ginger root

Place all the ingredients together in a teapot and stir to mix. Pour hot water over the herbs, 2 teaspoons per cup, and let steep for 5 minutes.

ECHINACEA ROOT TEA

Every herb store or organic grocer will have dried echinacea root for fighting colds and negating respiratory infections. It is an amazing immune booster. Just mince a teaspoonful and steep in a cup (240ml) of boiling water. Sweeten to taste and drink at least a couple of cups a day.

A good night's sleep

Sleep plays an essential role in keeping our immune systems strong, and studies have shown that good-quality sleep can boost the T cells in our bodies that fight off infection. During the winter it's especially important to get a good night's sleep to help you stay well and fight off seasonal illnesses. Try the following essential oils which can help to bring peaceful sleep.

Agrimony

Used since ancient times, this oil is very highly regarded as an all-purpose healer for the body. Helpful with sleep, it is a protective herb which brings about a sense of wellbeing and ease.

Anise

This carries a strong scent of licorice and has a wide variety of usages. It is excellent for renewed vitality, and can be applied topically in combination with carrier oils for therapeutic massage. It also makes for deep, peaceful sleep and protects against nightmares.

Caraway

This strengthens mental alertness and enhances memory. Caraway essential oil will empower visionary dreams if you sprinkle a couple of drops on your pillowcase at night before sleep.

Mimosa

This oil will help you relax and can even bring deep, dream-filled sleep. Mimosa has a lightly honeyed scent and has a very important aspect in that it will abet self-esteem and self-love. Try mimosa in a steam bath or as a perfume you wear to imbue and surround yourself with a sense of self-worth.

Rosewood

Great for easing its user into a restful night's sleep, this oil can be used to calm restlessness and overcome the blues. It has a very balancing energy, can aid burnout, helps with renewal, and brings a youthful feeling.

Spruce

Sometimes referred to as Black Spruce, this woody and rich oil can promote mental clarity for its user. It is also very grounding for when you feel scattered. It was long used as a medicinal by Indigenous Americans who valued the positive effects to mind, body, and spirit. Smelling the scent in a mist or diffuser can aid breathing, relax you, and help you sleep. You can also use it for purification rituals, as did the Indigenous Americans.

Valerian

Originally from Europe and Asia, this oil engenders an overall feeling of relaxation in its user. It can be used to deter restlessness, promote a full night's rest, and is a great and nurturing aroma for girls and women. Valerian is also an anointing oil and is said to bring luck to your endeavors. It was especially popular during medieval times, when it was regarded as a major healing herb for many maladies.

Sweet dreams tea

Ideal for cold winter nights, this tea will also help you go to sleep after
a stressful day or when suffering from insomnia.

**2oz (50g) dried
elder flowers**

2oz (50g) dried lavender

**2oz (50g) dried
hawthorn flowers**

**2oz (50g) dried
hops flowers**

**2oz (50g) dried
valerian leaves**

2oz (50g) dried basil leaves

Mix everything together. Use about three pinches
to make a large cup of tea; infuse in boiling water
and strain off the herbs. Drink about 45 minutes
prior to bedtime.

Sleep milk

Enhance the dreamy vibes on a chilly evening with this soothing milk drink.
The ghee is grounding and nourishing, which is perfect right before sleep.

1 teaspoon ghee

**½ tablespoon
ashwagandha powder**

**½ tablespoon mucuna
pruriens powder**

**½ teaspoon
astragalus powder**

**1½ cups (350ml)
warm almond milk
(or other nut milk)**

1 teaspoon raw honey

Serves 1

Heat the ghee in a saucepan over a low heat
for 1 minute, then add the herbs and simmer for
30 seconds. Add the milk and stir. (If you have a
hand-held milk frother or whisk, you may use it to
froth the milk.) Remove from the heat. Once the liquid
has cooled to a warm temperature, add the honey.

Deep sleep ritual

If you have slept poorly recently, reset with this simple and powerful ritual.

7 dried lavender stalks

small muslin bag

7-inch (18-cm) piece of ribbon

rosewood essential oil

Right before you get into bed, place the lavender stalks into the bag. Take the ribbon and sprinkle it with rosewood oil seven times. Tie the muslin bag with the ribbon. Hold the bag in both hands and crush it slightly, so the lavender releases its tranquil fragrance. Then speak aloud:

On this and every night,
Deep rest is within sight.
Each morning, I will awaken to light
Each day, my energy is fresh and bright.
And so it is; so it will be.

Place the muslin bag under your pillow and you will sleep deeply and awaken refreshed and restored.

SLEEP POSY

For another way to infuse your bedroom with healing, calming scents, gather 10 sprigs each of lavender and rosemary in a bunch and tie with a ribbon. Hang the posy from a bedpost or leave on your nightstand.

Soothing remedies

Sometimes it's impossible to avoid seasonal illnesses during the cold months. From teas and soups to breathing exercises, these healing remedies will soothe you when you're feeling run-down, boost your immune system, and help to get you back to full health.

Immunity essence

This homemade healing oil brings an instant immune system boost. As soon as you feel slightly under the weather, one application should make a difference.

¼ cup (10g) dried rosemary

¼ cup (10g) crushed sandalwood chips

¼ cup (10g) fresh carnation petals

mortar and pestle

sealable colored glass jar

extra-virgin olive oil

Crush the rosemary, sandalwood, and carnation petals in the mortar. Transfer the crushed herbs to the jar and fill it with olive oil, making sure to cover the herbs. Store for seven days on a windowsill where the jar will be exposed to both the sun and moon. Strain the oil, then return the infused oil to the jar.

You now have a hearty supply of oil to use in the bath, or to rub on your pulse points: on your temples, wrists, neck, and behind the ears.

THE BENEFITS OF ROSEMARY

Rosemary contains lots of iron and vitamin C, making it a great ingredient to include in recipes or teas during the cold months of the year. It also helps to alleviate muscle pain, reduce anxiety, and aid sleep.

Soothing scents

Banish winter colds and coughs or keep them at bay with this sweet-smelling respiratory aid.

10 drops rosemary essential oil

10 drops tea tree essential oil

10 drops eucalyptus essential oil

10 drops lavender essential oil

1 teaspoon sea salt

Shake all the oils and salt together in a small bottle, then hold the open container in both hands under your nose and breathe in deeply three times.

You can also administer this respiratory booster via a vaporizer or bath. Mix the oils only, without the salt, and add four drops to the water of a vaporizer or diffuser or a cotton ball tucked into your pillowcase, or pour six drops into the running water of a hot bath.

Breathing practice for healing

This breathing practice can be used to address lung issues in the winter such as minor colds, as well as asthma, bronchitis and more, or as a daily practice for healthy lungs. Lung ailments, whether chronic or temporary, have many, varying causes including exposure to pollutants, allergies, and multiple chemical sensitivity (MCS), and some people are more predisposed to them than others.

One aspect not to be overlooked is the mind–body connection. If breath is life, the lungs are the sacred chambers where our feelings about life dwell. When the lungs are out of balance, it may be a result of fear of life, grief, depression, small hurts, or feelings of being overwhelmed. The lungs and heart are roommates, and therefore the emotions that relate to the heart (unconditional love, balance, harmony, courage) can be "picked up" by the lungs and, when there is an imbalance, manifest into various respiratory ailments. If we are experiencing grief, fear, heartbreak, overwhelm, and a lack of unconditional love, our inspiration to live and our ability to breathe may be adversely affected. It's as if we cannot take life in, which shows up as congestion and shortness of breath. On the other hand, if we are feeling great and catch a chest cold or worse, the inability to receive enough oxygen can have a dour effect on our emotional experience since struggling for air is exhausting and frightening.

When the breath is taken away and given back, it's like the gift of life returned in 3D Technicolor. Visualize that your lungs are filled with branches and leaves extending from your sternum. They glow and quiver as the breeze of your breath cleanses and nourishes. This practice purifies, relaxes, and rejuvenates the lungs.

If you are very congested and have difficulty breathing, practice the Breath Awareness technique. If not, practice Ujjayi.

Breath awareness

This is simply becoming aware of your breath and holding that attention on purpose. Gently but firmly direct your attention, as many times as it takes, with patience, toward your breath. Feel the sensation of the breath in your body, wherever you notice it, as it comes and goes through your nose. You may find it helpful to direct your focus to a specific area, such as your belly or chest or nostrils. You do not need to alter your breath but simply observe your natural breathing and passively allow your thoughts to

move along without attaching to any particular thought for any length of time. Instead attach your mind to your breath.

Ujjayi (triumphant or victorious) breath

Do a minimum of 10 of these breaths. Continue for as long as you are inspired.

This breath practice, which is generally referred to by the Sanskrit name, builds upon Breath awareness but adds sound and action to hold your attention more firmly to the breath and the present moment. In this way, you "triumph" over the chatter of the mind. It is the most common breath used in a yoga class to help you to deepen your concentration and to achieve a greater mind–body connection. This can facilitate more depth, progress, and healing. On your inhale "hug" or slightly constrict your throat so that it sounds like wind in a tunnel or "whoosh" and on your exhale, push the breath out through the same "hug" in the back of your throat. It should feel as if you are breathing in and out of a nose in your throat rather than your nostrils. These breaths are longer and deeper than your natural breath.

THE HEALING POWER OF HONEY

As well as being rich in nutrients, raw honey is rich in cancer-fighting phytonutrients and powerful anti-oxidants which are found in the propolis that the bees use to sterilize the beehive.

Oxymel tonic

This tonic dates back to ancient times and is made of two seemingly opposing ingredients—honey and vinegar. Herbs can be added to great effect and when you see honey-menthol cough drops on the pharmacy shelf, note their 2,000-year-old origins. Oxymels are supremely effective for respiratory issues.

herbs—any from the following: oregano, elder flower, sage, balm, mint, lemon peel, thyme, lavender, rose petals, hyssop, or fennel

honey

vinegar

Place your chosen herbs into a canning jar, then pour over equal parts honey and vinegar. Store in a dark cupboard and give the sealed jar a good shake every day. After two weeks, strain out the herbs through cheesecloth and store in the fridge.

Drink a tablespoon of tonic for relief from your symptoms. You can also cook with the oxymel or add it to tea.

Cough teas

Simple teas can have powerful healing effects. The two tea recipes below can combat colds and coughs—try both to see which taste you prefer.

Recipe 1

2oz (50g) dried sage

2oz (50g) dried marjoram

10 star anise

2oz (50g) dried coltsfoot

honey or molasses, to taste

Recipe 2

2oz (50g) dried thyme

2oz (50g) dried verbena

2oz (50g) dried fennel

2oz (50g) dried mullein flowers

honey or molasses, to taste

Mix together all the ingredients. Use three pinches of the mixture for a large cup of tea, add boiling water, and let it steep for 5–10 minutes. Strain out the herbs, then sweeten with honey or molasses if desired.

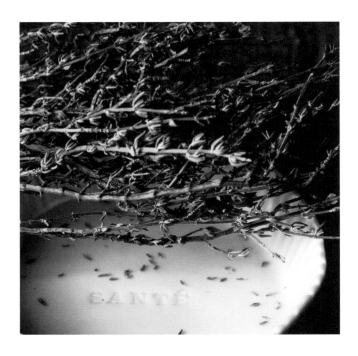

Fever tea

This tea helps break a fever, ease rheumatism, and strengthen the constitution after an illness.

¾oz (20g) dried
thyme flowers

¾oz (20g) dried
holly leaves

¾oz (20g) dried
elder flowers

¾oz (20g) dried
lime flowers

¾oz (20g) dried
meadowsweet

honey or molasses,
to taste

Mix together all the ingredients. Use about three pinches to make a large cup of tea. Infuse in boiling water and strain off the herbs. Sweeten with honey or molasses if desired.

SOOTHING MEADOWSWEET

Meadowsweet has been used as a traditional treatment for soothing colds and nausea, and like aspirin it contains salicylic acid.

Icelandic lamb soup (Kjötsúpa)

This rustic, simple soup uses lamb or mutton and root vegetables. It has legendary healing powers and is perfect for a dark winter's night. The meat is braised and creates its own stock. Traditional cultures have always included bones, tendons, and cartilage in their soups, and this health-giving recipe provides calcium, collagen, and glycine.

18oz (500g) rutabaga/ swede, peeled

18oz (500g/4 medium-sized) potatoes, peeled

9oz (250g/4 medium-sized) carrots, peeled

piece of leek/a few parsnips, peeled (optional)

35oz (1kg) lamb on the bone, such as shoulder

1 tablespoon Icelandic salt or sea salt, plus extra for seasoning (Icelandic salt is the least contaminated on earth, so it's worth finding)

½ teaspoon or few sprigs each oregano and thyme

half an onion, finely chopped

3½oz (100g) cabbage, sliced, or kale

⅓ cup (80g) rice or ⅓ cup (30g) rolled oats, if you would like a heartier soup

freshly ground black pepper

Serves 4–6

Trim the fat off the lamb and cut it into a few pieces. Cut the rutabaga or swede, potatoes, carrots, and leek or parsnips (if using) into similar size chunks. Make sure they aren't too small.

In a large pot, brown the lamb all over on a medium– high heat. Pour in 1¾ pints (1.5l) water, or enough to just cover the meat, and bring to the boil. Use a spoon to skim the scum off the top and add the tablespoon of salt and the rice or oats, if using.

Add the herbs and onion, simmer for another 50 minutes, then add the swede, potatoes, carrots, and leek or parsnips (if using), and simmer for another 20 minutes until they are soft.

Remove the meat and the bones from the soup, roughly chop the meat, and return to the pot. Season to taste with salt and pepper. Serve with bread and butter.

Ginger and carrot soup

Ginger is an energetic herb and adds fire and spice to anything it is used for, whether a healing cup of tea, a salad, a savory dish, or this special soup. Ginger root helps to soothe the symptoms of colds, congestion, flu, and fever. Combine it with carrots, which are wonderfully grounding, and you have a simple, comforting winter soup.

1 lb (450g) carrots, cleaned and sliced; set aside the carrot greens

4 cups (900ml) water

1 tablespoon fresh ginger, chopped

1 large garlic clove, peeled and crushed

¼ teaspoon crushed red pepper, plus extra to garnish

½ teaspoon salt

1 lemon

Serves 6

Put the carrots in a big pot and add the water. Bring to a boil, then simmer on a medium heat for 20–25 minutes, adding the ginger, garlic, red pepper, and salt after 5 minutes.

When the carrots are tender, transfer them with their water to a blender and blend until smooth. Stir in several squeezes of lemon juice and pour into bowls or mugs. Garnish with a few chopped carrot greens and a sprinkling of crushed red pepper.

Almond and eucalyptus bath

For thousands of years, we humans have been "taking the waters" as a way to restore, and also heal illness. Try this bath recipe as a way to simultaneously warm you up on a cold night, and relax and soothe you during an illness.

4 cups (720g) Epsom salts

½ cup (120ml) almond oil

6 drops comfrey essential oil

4 drops eucalyptus essential oil

4 drops rosemary essential oil

6 drops bergamot essential oil

Pour the salts into a large glass bowl and fold in the carrier oil. Now add in the essential oils, stirring after each is added. Continue to blend the mixture until it is moistened thoroughly. You can add more almond oil if necessary.

When your bathtub is one-quarter full, add one-quarter of the salt mixture under the faucet (tap). Breathe in deeply ten times, inhaling and exhaling fully.

When the tub is full, step inside and exercise your breath ten more times. Use the rest of the salts to scrub your body, carefully avoiding your eye area. Rest and rejuvenate as long as you like while visualizing your renewed health and vigor.

Breath for sinus trouble

Sinus problems are often particularly bad during the winter, when the cold weather and change in humidity can irritate the sinuses and lead to headaches, congestion, and a loss of your sense of smell, as well as other symptoms. When we experience temporary or chronic anosmia (loss of the sense of smell) our quality of life can be severely diminished. The olfactory sense is closely linked to memory, comfort, joy, and even our sense of safety. It may not be as apparent as the other four senses, but it can definitely leave a void. That's not even to mention the discomfort and pressure of sinus headaches due to inflammation in the tissue lining of the mucous membranes.

Whatever the reason, when our sinuses are clogged, so are we. When the sweet moment of stopping for a flower or inhaling the aroma of our favorite dish eludes us, life can be a little flat. We may also experience brain fog and facial pain, feel sluggish and isolated, and lose our appetites or enjoyment of food. Sinus trouble can stem from a cold, allergies, environmental sensitivities, swimming, flying, dry air, a deviated septum, or reaction to medication and cancer treatments, to name a handful of causes.

Although it may sound counterintuitive to practice breathing when you can't even get a decent regular breath of air, quite often the right breath will do the trick in dislodging the blockage in your nose. This Skull Shining Breath exercise will bring you light and movement. Stress and overly busy lives can make us more susceptible to sinus trouble in all its forms so pause and take in some deep healing breaths with this practice.

Skull shining breath

This technique is used for clearing, cleansing and purifying, and revitalizing. It is most commonly done seated although can also be done standing up. This practice is not recommended during pregnancy or for those with hypertension or panic disorder. Substitute with Ujjayi Breath (see page 53) for 1–3 minutes. Place your hands on your belly or rest them on your legs. Inhale fully through your nose and exhale through your mouth. On your next inhale, stop short of a full breath and exhale through your nose with a forceful blow as your abdomen engages toward your navel. Let your inhale follow naturally. Focus on the exhale, which comes from the action of the belly pulling in. The inhale is a slower, natural reaction to the force of the exhale. Both breaths are

done through the nose. It sounds a bit like a train chugging along or the piston of an engine. To start with, practice 3 rounds of 11 breaths with 2 or 3 natural breaths in between. Pause between each round and hold the breath in for 8–15 seconds before exhaling completely and beginning the next round. You may eventually increase to 3 rounds of 27 breaths.

Chapter 3

Caring for Your Body, Mind, and Soul

Our physical and emotional health can suffer during the winter, so it's essential to practice self-care at this time of year. This chapter includes lots of ways of taking care of your mind, body, and spirit, helping you not just to combat the winter blues, but also to thrive during the coldest season. Nurture yourself with breathing techniques to address fatigue, joint pain, and more; try a self-massage practice, and treat your body to soothing baths and skincare recipes.

Tuning in to your body

Starting with a simple ritual to allow you to focus on your health, here you'll find self-care practices to help you look after your body and boost your wellbeing through the coldest season.

Wellbeing ritual

As the seasons change from fall to winter, it is helpful to bring awareness of taking care of your wellbeing to every day of your life. A regular ritual for your health can in time become a daily ritual.

You could adorn one of your favorite home spaces with fresh flowers and candles in colors that represent healing: yellow, red, and green. Every morning for seven days, light the candles and contemplate your future self in an optimal state of health, while you repeat these words:

Today I arise on this glorious day

Under this rising sun, hear me say:

I will walk in wellness in every way

For body, mind, and soul, I pray.

Blessed be, and may it be so.

Your healing intention

Think about what you need before you try the self-care practices in this chapter. Your reason is your intention, and is the focus of your ritual; holding this in mind will direct your personal energy. One basic guideline is that the creation of ritual should be not only for you and your loved ones, but also "for the greater good." Some examples of reasons include:

• To bring renewed health to body and spirit

• To bless a personal space or family home

• To bless and bring calm and contentment to the people in your life

• To bring about a more peaceful community and world

Breathing practice for fatigue

It stands to reason that we can become exhausted from mental or physical exertion or illness. This could be when we are under duress, overworked, have fallen ill, encounter major life changes, hormonal fluctuations, or insomnia, experience mental disturbances, have poor nutrition, lack exercise, and so on.

But our life force can also be drained if our work/life is lacking luster, we feel estranged in our community, and our relationships are stale. We can be especially susceptible to this in the winter, when the cold weather can take a toll on our mood and tempt us to stay at home and isolate ourselves from family and friends.

In yoga and Ayurveda (the sister science and whole-health system from India) the whole person and all aspects of life are examined when there is imbalance. Under this paradigm, if we are soldiering on feeling a lack of purpose and meaningful connections, our entire internal eco-system can be thrown off. Humans are pack animals and as such need a place in the order of things that matter. If we don't have that, we may grow uninspired and very tired. Tedium can be torturous.

Whatever the root cause of your fatigue, it's always a good idea to take a wide-angle approach. In addition to the basics of food, sleep, and exercise, what interests and excites you? Instead of just making it through the winter by following your normal routine, is there call for a new experience or hobby? Is there room for growth in your work? Are you engaged in community? The eternal now is a perfect moment to assess, reboot, and perhaps rebirth some aspect of your life. You can make a tiny shift in habits or you can go massive. Whether you're short on sleep or soul searching, a perfect start is to incorporate this sunny mood-enhancing and energy-boosting practice.

Sun breath

There's nothing like the energy of the sun to make you feel alive. This breath will bring a shot of sunshine to your soul during the darkest months of the year. Practice for 5–10 rounds minimum.

Sometimes called Right Nostril Breathing, this breathing technique can cultivate perseverance, enthusiasm, and zeal, and renew your hope. From a seated position, place your left hand on your thigh. Fold the index and middle finger of your right hand into your palm leaving the thumb, ring finger, and pinky fingers free. (This is called Vishnu Mudra.) You can do this with your left hand if you are left-handed. Close your left nostril with your ring finger and inhale through the right nostril.

Then gently pinch both nostrils shut, using the thumb on the right nostril, and pause for a few seconds with both nostrils closed.

Lift the ring finger from the left nostril and exhale through it. Continue so that you always inhale through the right and exhale through the left.

Self-massage

A great way of nurturing your body and practicing self-care during the winter, Abhyanga is a form of massage that is viewed as a medicinal therapy. The Sanskrit word abhyanga means "oil massage." It's been shown to provide deep nourishing and cleansing effects on the entire bodily system.

Traditionally, this lymphatic massage is performed by two practitioners working in sync with each other. However, the practice can also be performed as a self-massage, which is just as beneficial and is considered to be one of the highest forms of healing.

Abhyanga is done by massaging warm herbal oil onto the entire body before bathing. It helps to nourish the tissues of the body; stimulates the organs; increases circulation; slows down aging; brings longevity; balances all three doshas; softens, clears, and increases firmness of the skin; helps combat insomnia; detoxes the lymphatic system; and clears the channels of the body. As well as being comforting and soothing during the coldest season, the heat of the massage stimulates neuropeptides in the skin and nourishes the body on a cellular level. Neuropeptides—small protein-like molecules—help neurons communicate with each other in specific ways. In the case of abhyanga, these neuropeptides stimulate the communication to heal the body.

CHOOSING AN OIL

The quality of the oil you use to massage your body matters. Avoid using low-quality and/or rancid oils because your skin will absorb every bit of any product you put on it. Jojoba oil is a good one to try, as it is gentle, moisturizing, and has healing properties.

How to practice self-massage

Here is an easy step-by-step guide to help you incorporate this ancient practice into your everyday self-care routine. The massage starts at the top of your head and works its way down the front and back of your body. You can oil just the top of your scalp or you may choose to oil your entire head, including your hair.

Remember to always test oils on a small patch of your skin to ensure you are not allergic before you apply the oil all over your body.

You will need:

4–8 fl oz (120–250ml) massage oil

heat-safe container, such as a ceramic, glass, or bpa-free plastic bowl

old towel

1 Warm the oil in a heat-safe container to a little warmer than body temperature. (Warming the oil in a double boiler/bain-marie on the stove will help you to manage the temperature more efficiently. You may also heat the oil in the microwave in 30-second increments, testing the temperature as you go.) To test the temperature of the oil, carefully apply a small spot of oil to your wrist to make sure it is not too hot.

2 Stand on an old towel in your bathroom—the towel will catch any excess oil so it doesn't stick to the floor.

3 Pour some oil into the palms of your hands, the more oil the better! Cover your entire body with the oil.

4 Using small circular strokes, massage the crown of your head. If you don't want oil in your hair, begin the massage at your ears. Avoid using the oil on your face, except for your ears and neck.

5 Using upward strokes and an open hand to create friction, massage the front and back of your neck.

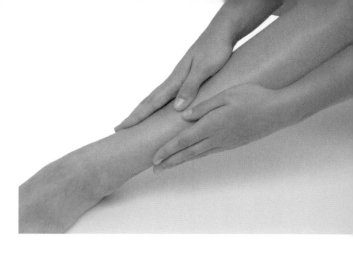

6 Using a clockwise circular motion, massage around your breasts/chest.

7 Using a clockwise circular motion, massage your stomach/abdominal area. You really need to work in deep here. If you are pregnant, recovering from surgery, or have chronic pain in this area, consult your specialist before deeply massaging the area.

8 Using long up and down strokes, rub one of your arms to create friction and heat. Once you have created heat, massage the entire arm with a circular motion, starting at the bottom of the wrist and working upward toward the heart on the inside of the arm. Repeat on the other arm.

9 Add some extra oil to your hands and, without straining, reach around to your back and spine and gently massage with up and down strokes.

10 Vigorously massage up and down your legs up to create friction and heat. Focus on the top of one thigh and work your way down the leg, taking care to work your hands in a circular motion on the insides of your legs (this is a huge lymphatic part and many toxins build up in these areas). Repeat on the other leg.

11 Take some extra time to focus on your feet. Really work the oil into your feet and don't leave a single toe untouched.

12 Once you've finished the massage, take a warm shower or bath for as long as feels comfortable. The idea is to open the pores to let the oil sink in deeper. Don't use soap to wash off the oil (it's not necessary). Towel dry after you shower or bathe. Take care when stepping out of the bathtub or shower, as the floor may be slippery.

Breathing practice for joint pain

Many people notice joint pain getting worse in the winter, and while the exact reasons for this aren't yet known, one theory is that the drop in temperature leads to the swelling of muscles and tendons. It's also thought that seasonal affective disorder (see page 26), which affects our mood, sleep, and energy, can lead to a higher perception of pain. There are numerous reasons for joint pain (also called arthralgia) including damage, disease, injury, bursitis, osteoarthritis, rheumatoid arthritis, surgery, and inflammation in the joints; one other cause isn't often discussed—stress inflammation. A gentle yoga practice can work wonders regardless of the diagnostic cause of the joint pain, but a special treasure trove of relief can be found by specifically addressing stress-related inflammation in the joints.

Stress has many triggers, but the kind that can become quite insidious, and often produces inflammation, is the low grade, chronic release of cortisol. Big traumatic events are not to blame for the relentless trickle of stress hormones into the system, but daily overwhelm, loneliness, isolation, or lack of community may be, and these issues can affect us especially during the coldest months of the year.

Chronic pain is another cause, and the subsequent shifts in your lifestyle to manage it. If you have lost mobility due to joint pain, you may feel the emotional wrench of no longer being able to take part in activities that brought you joy and the kinship of those with whom you shared your passions. This kind of stress can cause or increase inflammation as the body tries to defend itself. To add fuel to the fire, less movement increases stiffness in the joints and aggravates inflammation in many cases. By expressing loving kindness toward yourself through a mindful breath practice, you can begin to relax and nourish your body.

This practice will stimulate your nadis (energy channels), which will lubricate your joints, increase your flexibility, and soothe your nervous system. A cooling breath relieves some of the hot pain of inflammation and intense emotions. Don't always practice alone. Share the magic by inviting friends or family to join you.

Cooling or hissing breath

Take up a comfortable, seated position either on a chair or on the floor, and practice between 10 and 30 rounds of this breath. If needed, rest at 10-round intervals.

Take a few deep breaths into your belly then form an "O" with your lips and slip your tongue through the opening, folding it to resemble a straw or tiny taquito. Wait until some saliva has formed and then breathe in through the "straw" (or bird's beak as the yogis saw it) drinking in the cool moisture. When you finish inhaling, close your lips and exhale completely through your nose. Continue with the breath for 3–5 minutes if possible. If you are not genetically predisposed to form a straw with your tongue, you can practice Hissing Breath, which is exactly the same practice but with a variation on the tongue position. For Hissing Breath, gently press your teeth together and open your lips so your teeth are exposed. Your tongue is folded back so the underside presses the roof of your mouth, resembling a quesadilla. Draw the moistened air in through the sides of your mouth and exhale through the nose.

Relieving digestive discomfort

Whether from comfort eating to get through the cold days, or indulging in more food than we're used to over the festive season, winter can take a toll on our digestive systems. If you have just eaten a large, poorly combined, and heavy meal, follow these tips to relieve yourself from discomfort.

• Take a gentle walk after the meal. Taking a short walk around the block will rev your metabolism, add an element of mobility, and break up heaviness from overeating. Don't go for a run—the aim is to get things moving in a downward flow, not to sweat out any toxins you've just eaten. You can save your sweat for a day later.

• The herbal formula Triphala (see pages 136–137) is a natural, rejuvenating detoxifier and purifier that is good to take nightly and it can also be handy to take when you have overindulged. It is made of three nourishing-support herbs: amalaki, bibhitaki, and haritaki. It promotes healthy weight loss and tones, nourishes, and strengthens the entire body. If taken after a meal, triphala will give your body a gentle cleanse, help remove any lingering toxicity formed by the food, and reset your digestion so you feel ready to go the next day.

• The mindset you are in while eating will affect the way you digest, process, and absorb your food. It's important to remember not to feel guilty or regret the things that you do. You can't change the past, only look toward the future for another chance to change. If eating certain food makes you feel awful, you'll inevitably learn that it's not in alignment with you to eat that food. However, it won't ruin your progress if you indulge during the festive season or decide to eat a cheeseburger, cake, burrito, or pizza once in a while. Focus on the good. Give thanks to your body, release guilt, and never regret. Life is about living and having fun so don't beat yourself up over the small stuff … especially food. Focus on being thankful, enjoy the quality of the time you have with loved ones during winter celebrations, and don't worry about the food.

Here are some more tips that will relieve digestive discomfort and help you stay balanced.

Warm water with fresh lemon juice

This drink is a great way of looking after your digestive system throughout the winter and holiday season. It should be drunk first thing in the morning to cleanse your bowels, promote digestion, and remove toxins.

1 lemon

1½–3¾ cups (350–900ml) water

½in (1-cm) piece of fresh ginger, peeled and grated (optional)

1 teaspoon raw honey (optional)

Serves 1

Wash the lemon and then either juice half of it or cut the lemon in half and squeeze some juice into a large mug. Add the ginger (if using) and rest of the lemon to the mug. Heat the water in a small saucepan on the stove until you see little bubbles forming at the bottom of the pan—do not let the water boil. Pour the warm water into the mug with the lemon juice.

Alternatively, if you don't have access to a stovetop, feel free to use a microwave. Heat the water in a microwave-safe cup (ceramic is preferred) in 30-second increments. Heating the water in a microwave for 40–50 seconds will usually warm the water to an enjoyable temperature. Stir in 1 teaspoon raw honey to the finished drink, if using.

Celery juice elixir

Drinking celery juice on an empty stomach helps to produce the stomach acid HCL, which breaks down proteins in the gut, restores electrolyte balance, detoxes the liver and kidneys, hydrates the skin, and lowers blood pressure. Celery is also an excellent source of natural sodium, which can help beat salty cravings when consumed daily.

1 bunch of celery, chopped

1 lemon, halved and peeled

Serves 1

Juice the celery and lemon. Alternatively, if you don't have a juicer, put the celery and lemon in a food processor or blender and blend on a high speed until well blended, then use a nut bag or cheesecloth (muslin) to strain the juice. Drink on an empty stomach for most benefits. The elixir will keep for up to 2 days in an airtight container or jar in the refrigerator.

THE FENNEL TRICK

At one time or another, most of us have eaten too much in one meal and instantly felt bloated. That's okay. Remember, lapses are bound to happen at some point. Luckily, there is an easy fix for a stuffed and bloated tummy: fennel. One of the simplest ways to incorporate it into your diet is to chew about 20 fennel seeds after a meal. Fennel helps to digest heavy sauces and carb-centric dishes, which is why you see a bowl of fennel seeds at the exit of most Indian restaurants. Drinking warm water will also help lessen the bloat.

Fennel, ginger, and lemon thyme reviver

Fennel can help improve the function of a poor, overworked, toxin-laden liver. It's also been called the pearl of aphrodisiacs, so it might really perk you up! Ginger should help wake up your senses and overcome nausea. Thyme helps soothe muscles and stomach at the same time.

1 teaspoon fennel seeds

1 thumbnail-sized piece of ginger, thinly sliced or grated

3 x 3-in (8-cm) long lemon thyme sprigs

boiling water

1 teaspoon honey, preferably raw, set, or runny

thyme sprig

spear of freshly peeled ginger

fennel floret

Serves 1

Place the fennel seeds, ginger, and sprigs of lemon thyme in the cup or heatproof glass. Pour over boiling water, almost to the top. Add the honey and stir. Garnish with a thyme sprig, ginger spear, and fennel floret.

Vitali-tea

This is a great tea to enjoy when you need to detox during the festive season. The liver and kidneys play an important role in keeping our bodies clean. When we support these two organs, we are aiding the body in the process of detoxification. Dandelion root is one of the best remedies for supporting the liver. It is also revered as a diuretic and can help reduce water retention. Licorice root supports the digestive system and helps push extra toxins out of our organs. Cinnamon and cardamom are warming, and orange peel is slightly heating and super rich in vitamin C, so this drink will help to boost your immune system during the winter, too.

1 tablespoon licorice root

1 tablespoon dandelion root

½ tablespoon dried orange peel

½ teaspoon cardamom seeds

¼ teaspoon cinnamon chips

2 cups (475ml) boiled water

raw honey, to taste

Serves 2

Put the herbs and boiled water in a bowl and let the mixture steep for 20 minutes. (Since we are working with roots, its best to let the tea steep for longer than we do when making teas with leaves or flowers.) Using a strainer or cheesecloth (muslin), strain the tea and pour into a thermos. Once the tea has cooled to a warm temperature, add the raw honey and enjoy!

Cut sugar cravings

Cardamom is one of the beautiful spices that is used in this book. If you happen to crave sweet things during the winter, specifically after eating a savory meal, chew on fresh cardamom seeds. This may sound strange but it actually works—it calms the nerves in the brain and diminishes the craving for something sweet.

Gentle detox tea

This age-old Ayurvedic recipe works wonders if you have been indulging a little too much during the holiday season. The fennel reduces bloating, the cumin helps to balance blood sugar, the coriander acts as a calming agent, and the manjistha is anti-inflammatory and clears the lymphatic system. Drink this tea daily if you're struggling regularly with constant gas, bloating, indigestion, acid reflux, or sluggish digestion. Daily use of this tea will not only promote a gentle full body detox but also facilitate fat burning and aid in the digestion of proteins.

4–5 cups (950ml–1.2 liters) water

½ teaspoon cumin seeds

½ teaspoon coriander seeds

½ teaspoon fennel seeds

½ teaspoon manjistha powder

Serves 4

Put the water in a saucepan and bring to the boil. Add the remaining ingredients, cover, and let boil for 5 minutes. Using a strainer or cheesecloth (muslin), strain the tea and pour into a thermos. Take small sips of the tea throughout the day or drink 1 cup (250 ml) of the tea before or after meals.

Breathing practice for digestion

Sometimes it's hard enough to have one brain, let alone two, and yet the belly is often called the "second brain." The brain and the gut are married, for better or worse, and their effect on each other runs both ways and quickly. The gastrointestinal (GI) tract is especially sensitive to our emotions connected to past, present, and future. Our language reinforces the physical sensations arriving from thoughts and feelings—"gut wrenching," "butterflies," "knots," "somersaults," "feeling nauseous." Digestive juices can even be released at the mere mention of a tantalizing meal hovering on the horizon. The connection that runs from brain to belly is clear. In reverse, dealing with GI issues can be depressing and produce anxiety and stress as we navigate pain, discomfort, and even bathroom schedules to accommodate this rollercoaster relationship. So we may need some guidance to find peace. But what causes this connection?

It is now widely understood among doctors, nutritionists, and scientists that having the right balance of healthy bacteria in your gut plays a key role in the healthy functioning of your GI tract, and your overall level of health and wellbeing. When under chronic stress due to any number of factors, including loss of loved ones, illness, financial issues, chronic anxiety, depression, panic disorder, mood disorders, addiction to name but a few, the fact is that our personal microbiome (collection of bacteria) does not function at top level.

Even generic daily stress can disturb the peace over time, as 80 percent of our immune system is located in the gut. When your system feels under siege, it can impact blood flow to your GI tract and the amount and type of good gut flora.

Healthy bacteria regulate cortisol (the stress hormone) and if they are compromised, the cortisol can run amok. As in any heated situation, this can cause inflammation. Inflammation means things are not working in unison or harmony— there is too much of something, which causes upset and imbalance. This practice is designed to bring things together (mind, body, and spirit/breath) and create a harmonious flow when we can allow our feelings to be heard without judgment and our bodies to relax into the *now*, stimulating healthy digestion on all levels. For this practice we balance the hot and cool to create the perfect climate for peace in body and mind.

Equal breath

We turn to Equal Breath to restore union and achieve balance. Aside from Breath Awareness, Equal Breath is the simplest of the breath techniques and is an excellent choice for stress reduction. Visualize yourself spreading your wings like a bird as you practice this breath, and feel free and at peace in this moment.

Lie on your back with your legs extended or bent at the knees with your feet on the ground. After a few moments of Breath Awareness (see page 52), begin to count to four in your mind as you inhale through your nose, then pause briefly and count to four silently as you exhale through your nose.

Do 4 rounds of the breath before relaxing for a few moments of natural breathing. Do another 4 rounds, and rest. Continue for as long as you like.

Healing baths

Taking a bath is deeply therapeutic, providing benefits for both your mind and body, as well as providing an instant warm-up when it's cold outside. Since time began, humans have been taking baths and in ancient cultures, bathing was revered as a holy act of self-love. The Romans built elaborate thermae, the ancient equivalent of the modern gym, with exercise rooms, massages, and heated water for cleaning and soaking. Many of these structures—the Baths of Caracalla in Rome, the eponymous Bath in England, and Varna in Bulgaria—still exist. Other cultures have followed suit, and the Japanese, Turks, and Swedes historically all had, and still have, elaborate bathing systems.

To bathe in nature, consider visiting a hot spring if you can. From Yellowstone National Park in the United States to the healing waters of Safaga, Egypt, Salar de Uyuni, Bolivia, or Antsirabe, Madagascar, immersion in warm, mineral-laden water has been shown to heal or ease muscle and joint pain, including arthritis, and to alleviate eczema and other skin conditions, and digestive disorders, especially when the water is rich in sulfur.

Sometimes baths are used to heal the spirit, and pilgrims trek to water sources across the globe. Devotees of the Virgin Mary journey to partake of spring water in Lourdes, France, which they believe will heal their ills; millions of Muslims stop at the Zamzam Well in Saudi Arabia while performing the hajj to Mecca; and Hindus seek out the Ganges River in India for spiritual purification. The ability of some these waters to heal us physically may come from their beneficial mineral content or soothing temperature, but no matter the pilgrim's destination or aspiration, there's something to be said for shared belief in a cure and a community directed toward a common effort.

Even if you can't travel, there are plenty of good things about taking a bath in the comfort of your own home. Immersing yourself in water can be relaxing—think a warm soak after a long day or when the weather is cold. It's commonly used after working out to prevent muscle stiffness, but it may also be an effective method of pain relief. Although more research is needed, it's possible that the shock of diving into cold water stimulates the sympathetic ("fight or flight") nervous system, causing the body to respond to the sensation of cold instead of to that of pain, thus providing relief. Perhaps by overshadowing the pain with this frigid blast, the cycle is broken. This could be especially helpful for nerve pain, which is notoriously difficult to treat.

It even turns out that hot baths may be a way to receive some of the positive benefits of exercise. Scientists at Loughborough University compared the impact of an hour-long soak in a hot bath (104°F/40°C) on metabolic fitness and calories burned with that of an hour of cycling. It turns out that although cycling burns more calories than bathing, the hot baths still resulted in the equivalent caloric output of a half-hour walk—about 140 calories! Hot baths also lowered blood sugar after eating and, more importantly, seemed to lower chronic inflammation, the body's response to infection, wounds, and diabetes.

Or you can try both. Alternating hot and cold baths is the foundation of a technique called contrast bathing, which is especially popular in Iceland and Scandinavia. The effect of immersing oneself in hot water and then cold, like having a cold dip after a sauna, is similar in principle to alternating hot and cold packs after an injury. The hot water increases blood flow throughout the body, while the cold constricts blood vessels, increasing local blood circulation in individual muscles. Alternating hot and cold may also increase lymphatic flow and even improve the function of the immune system.

Some of this positive effect isn't from the temperature at all, but from the gentle pressure of being under water, so choose whichever method works best for you.

Relaxing bath recipes

Treat your physical and emotional body with kindness during the winter by slowing down and taking time to bathe. If you don't have a bathtub, you can use the recipes provided here in a footbath instead. You can adjust the quantities of the ingredients to the amount of water you are using or make the footbath more potent by leaving the recipes as they are. Make sure the water in the footbath comes up to your ankles.

Salt scrub to relax and aid sleep

This bath soak is marvelous for aromatic relaxation. The blend swiftly delivers serenity and a combination of full relaxation and heightened awareness. Magnesium flakes are easily available from health-food stores and pharmacies.

handful of fresh mint leaves

½ cup (3½oz/100g) Epsom salts

½ cup (3½oz/100g) Himalayan pink salt

1 cup (7oz/200g) magnesium flakes

1 tablespoon Roman chamomile essential oil

12 drops lavender essential oil

4 drops neroli essential oil

While you run a hot bath, crush the mint leaves in your hand and toss them directly into the hot water pouring from the faucet (tap). Now place all the salts in a metal bowl and gently fold in the magnesium flakes. Lastly, add the essential oils and stir lightly. Now pour half of the mixture under the faucet and when the bath is ready, disrobe and step in. Sit back and enjoy the delightful scent of the fresh mint and aromatherapy salts and oils. After a few minutes, take a loofah or a rough washcloth and use the remaining mix to scrub your skin. Afterward, sit for a spell and enjoy the stimulating sensations.

MARVELOUS MAGNESIUM

The magnesium actually slows the production of the stress hormone in your body and aids sleep, as well as being marvelous for your skin.

SOOTHING SALT

Salt is known for its ability to trap negative energy and clear it from a person, space, or object. Epsom salt is the most basic and potent salt you can add to your bath. Epsom salts reduce stress, eliminate toxins, and decrease pain, inflammation, and bloat.

Detox bath

These invigorating bath salts help to draw toxins out of the body and soften the skin.

2 cups (450g) Epsom salts

1 cup (225g) baking soda (bicarbonate of soda)

10 drops of ginger essential oil

1 large lemon, washed and sliced

Makes enough for 1 use

Fill your bathtub with warm water and then add all the ingredients. Soak in the bath for 20–60 minutes.

Rose milk bath

You couldn't dream up a more luxurious bath for your skin than this concoction. The lactic acid in the milk helps to remove dead skin, while the rose oil calms and tones new skin.

1½ cups (190g) milk powder (raw if available)

½ cup (130g) Himalayan pink salt

1 handful dried or fresh rose petals

10 drops of rose essential oil

Makes enough for 1 use

Put all the ingredients except the rose petals in a bowl of warm water and stir until the milk powder and salt dissolve. Fill your bathtub with water, then add the milk and salt mixture and sprinkle in the rose petals. Soak in the bath for 20–60 minutes.

Moisturizing coconut bath

Coconut milk creates a rich, moisturizing bath and leaves skin silky smooth. Ylang ylang is a heady, exotic scent that is lightened and heightened by the citrusy note of the orange.

2 drops ylang ylang essential oil

3 drops orange essential oil

1 can (14 fl oz/400ml) of coconut milk

Makes enough for 1 use

Combine the essential oils with the coconut milk and add to a tubful of warm water.

Seasonal skincare

The winter can play havoc on our complexions, as the cold and dry air makes it difficult for our skin to stay moisturized. Use these recipes to pamper yourself and keep your skin healthy over the winter months.

Blissful massage bars

Treat your skin during the winter with these luxurious and beautifully scented massage bars. Cocoa butter is beloved for its delicious chocolate scent, but you could also use sumptuous shea butter or mango butter. Use your favorite essential oil to create a scent you will love.

3oz (80g) beeswax

½ cup (120ml) almond oil

3oz (80g) cocoa butter

1 teaspoon essential oil of your choice

Heat the beeswax, almond oil, and cocoa butter slowly in a bain-marie or double boiler (a small heatproof bowl set over a saucepan of simmering water) over a low heat until just melted. Remove from the heat and let cool slightly. Stir in the essential oil. Pour the mix into soap bar molds and let cool for about 2 hours, until hardened. Place in the freezer for a few minutes to make it easier to pop the bars out of the molds. To use, rub the massage bar onto the skin—the warmth of your body will immediately begin to melt the bar.

Skin-nourishing body whip

Lather this decadent mixture all over your skin as you get into the bathtub, then ease down into the water and just soak. It is fabulously luxurious and will nourish your skin wonderfully.

1 cup (220g) virgin coconut oil (which is solid at room temperature)

4 drops essential oil of your choice

Put the coconut oil in a medium-sized bowl. Using a hand mixer or an electric mixer with a whisk attachment, whip the oil until it reaches a soft consistency, like whipped cream. Add essential oil and whip to combine. Use every bit for your treatment; you deserve it.

Raspberry lip balm

Once you have all the right ingredients it's very easy to make your own lip balm—and once you start, you'll never go back to the store-bought variety. Beeswax is the key ingredient; it's completely natural, it makes the lip balm stay hard, and it's an excellent lip protector and moisturizer during the cold days of winter. There are also some extra moisturizing ingredients, in the form of vitamin E oil and jojoba oil, to take good care of your lips. The raspberries give your lips a slight hint of pink the natural way.

1½ tablespoons freeze-dried raspberries

2 tablespoons pure jojoba oil

1½ teaspoons natural beeswax pellets (see note)

10 drops pure vitamin E oil

1 drop rose or lavender essential oil (optional)

Grind the freeze-dried raspberries in a coffee grinder or small food processor until very fine. Gently heat the jojoba oil and beeswax together in a double boiler (a small heatproof bowl set over a saucepan of simmering water), or in a microwave on its lowest setting for a few seconds. When melted, remove from the heat and add the vitamin E oil, raspberry powder, and, if you wish, a drop of rose or lavender essential oil. Pour the mixture into a 1½-oz (45ml) jar with a lid and leave to set. It keeps for up to a month. The raspberry powder can feel a bit grainy on the lips, but rub your lips together and use it like an exfoliant to leave your lips feeling super-soft.

Note: It is easier to buy beeswax in pellet form, as the blocks are difficult to cut for small quantities.

Chamomile face mask

Warm oatmeal and chamomile tea conjure up a soothing feeling just at the thought of them—and they can also be an important part of your beauty regime.

up to 1 cup (225ml) chamomile tea, steeped for a half hour

1 tablespoon honey

1 teaspoon baking soda (bicarbonate of soda)

½ cup (50g) old-fashioned oats, ideally steel cut, crushed using a fork or ricer

2 tablespoons brown sugar

Put half a cup (110 ml) of chamomile tea in a small bowl and add the honey, baking soda (bicarbonate of soda), and oats. Add 2 tablespoons more tea to create an oaty paste. Set aside for 5 minutes. If the mixture is too dry, you can get the desired texture by adding a little more tea. Add the sugar and mix well.

Apply the face mask to clean, damp skin. Allow it to dry for 10 minutes, then rinse off thoroughly and massage your face gently with a natural moisturizer. Your skin will be miraculously smooth!

Glowing goddess face oil

Excellent for soothing and moisturizing your skin when the weather is cold and harsh, this face oil is suitable for all skin types. You can use it as a daily moisturizer, serum, or at any moment when you're in need of some self-love.

2 tablespoons jojoba oil

1 tablespoon sea buckthorn oil

1 tablespoon carrot seed oil

1 tablespoon tamanu oil

1 teaspoon rose hip oil

20–30 drops hyaluronic acid

2 drops of geranium essential oil

2 drops of frankincense essential oil

2 drops of lavender essential oil

2 drops of sandalwood essential oil

Makes about 4 fl oz (120ml)

Mix all the ingredients together in a small bowl. Using a funnel, transfer the oil to a 4-fl-oz (120-ml) glass jar or bottle. Store in a cool, dark place.

This oil will keep for up to 6 months. Massage your face daily with the oil to enhance your skin's radiance and keep it supple.

Breathing practice for healthy, glowing skin

We can use this breath to enhance the health and beauty of the skin during the harsh winter season. It is also a way of releasing limiting beliefs you might have about your skin.

Your skin is the one outfit you can never change, and yet it changes constantly throughout your life. It's the town crier of life's passages. Skin is also not great at keeping secrets, such as lack of sleep, too many cocktails, or poor hydration hygiene. It is the spiritual gift that keeps on giving, as it can be a lesson in self-acceptance and the celebration of our individuality.

Our skin can also cause us to judge ourselves in a way that is damaging and divisive. One avenue toward a healthier relationship with your skin is to focus on its multiple and essential purposes (see below).

Bellows Breath aids in digestion and detoxification through the skin. It provides a gorgeous glow that surpasses any perceived flaws as your breath cleans and balances the whole organism.

What skin does

• It keeps our bodies together.

• It regulates our temperature and protects us from germs, toxins, and the elements.

• Perhaps one of the best things, but least considered, is that it gives us sensation. Our skin allows us to *feel*.

• Through skin we absorb the things we need and secrete the things we need to get rid of from the body.

Bellows breath

Follow the instructions on opposite, or, if you are pregnant, suffer from hypertension or panic disorder, or feel dizzy or unwell, skip this breath and substitute with Ujjayi Breath for 1–3 minutes (see page 53). Continue with 3 sets of Bellows Breath or 10–30 rounds of Alternate Nostril Breath.

It is best for beginners to practice Bellows Breath sitting down, but those who are more experienced in breathing practices could do it standing up. In kundalini yoga, it is even practiced in certain poses. To begin, take a few breaths in and out through your nose, noticing your belly expand on the inhale and contract on the exhale. Inhale a natural half-breath, then begin Bellows Breath by exhaling forcefully through your nose and inhaling at the same rate, which is quick—about one cycle per second. The inhale and exhale are even in tempo and intensity. Your body is still and straight except for the pumping action in your diaphragm. Begin with 10 rounds and rest for 3–5 natural breaths in between. Then work up to 20 rounds and then 30 rounds with the resting breaths in between. If you feel lightheaded or dizzy, relax and breathe naturally and stay with 10 pumps at a time for 3 rounds.

Chapter 4

Revitalizing, Recharging, and Renewing

Whether you want to set new goals at the start of the winter, revitalize your routine during the long dark months, or reset for the new year, this chapter includes lots of ways to give your mental and physical health a boost. Care for your body and mind by staying active, and find tips on mindful eating as well as recipes for energizing teas. To help you thrive at this time of year, there's also a section on how to create a healthy and calming daily routine, as well as advice on shifting your mindset through positive affirmations.

Energizing through exercise

It's difficult to stay active and move your body daily when you are busy taking care of kids, working long hours at a desk, spending time with family, or just overall trying to do it all. Combined with these demands, the cold, dark months of winter make it especially hard to motivate yourself to create new exercise habits. However, movement is vital for your health (not just your physical health but also your mental health), so instead of looking at movement—whether it be yoga, the gym, sports, dance, classes, and so on—as a chore, try thinking about moving your body as a form of self-love. The more we love ourselves, the more we thrive.

Every day you have an opportunity to honor your body by nourishing it, moving it, and loving it. When you stay active and keep your body moving in an organic way that is a natural complement to the energetics of your body, you will find that life flows with more ease and less stress. As well as lifting your mood and energy during the winter, movement is a huge part of longevity and living a balanced life. When you move your body you are treating yourself with the respect you deserve. Your body deserves to be treated right 100 percent of the time, no matter the season or the weather.

You may find it difficult to stay motivated when it comes to daily movement but doing at least 10 minutes of designated yoga or any other activity will really help your mind–body connection and create more space for healing.

Movement can be done anywhere, at any time; every little bit you do counts!
Here are five ways to stay active:

• Stretch, dance, jump around, and move as soon as you wake up in the morning:
Five minutes is all you need. This not only gets your energy up for the day, but also
wakes up all your body parts.

• Walk or bike to work: Doing some movement before you start work will increase
your focus and prolong your energy. If your work is too far away to walk or bike,
park your car further away from your place of work and walk the longest distance
possible to get there.

• Stop, drop, and stretch: Try to take a 2-minute break from work every hour to move
your body in an organic way. This will help you feel motivated and ready to work again.
You don't only have to stretch, you could do push-ups, crunches, squats, planks,
dance—whatever feels right to you.

• Take a break: Whether you work from home or elsewhere, you can add movement
into your post-lunchtime routine. Light movement, such as walking, is helpful for
digestion after you have eaten. Either walk to a park to eat your lunch and then
walk back or take a walk around the block after you eat. If it's very cold outside
and you work in an office, just take a walk up and down the stairs if you don't
want to go outdoors.

• Do activities with friends: It's much easier to stay motivated when you have a partner
to help keep you accountable. Suggest going for a walk instead of meeting for tea to
chat. Instead of going out to a bar, go to a salsa or Zumba class and shake your hips.
There are plenty of fun activities you can do with others that will keep you connected
while moving together.

Cold therapy

Going for walks on crisp, cold days reminds us where our "edges" are—there is a physical sensation of "you" and "weather" that is not experienced in quite the same way during more clement times. Likewise, walking in winter is usually more challenging, bringing us not just to a temperature "edge" but to the edge of our physical ability. It is in those edges where growth comes—not only in terms of stamina, but in our understanding of our place as we move through the world.

Cold exposure, such as ice baths and cold showers, is on trend these days—and there is a reason for it, as the physiological and psychological benefits are many. As well as improving circulation, exposure to cold temperatures can activate the body's stress response, triggering the release of happy endorphins, and increasing feelings of wellbeing and even euphoria.

The act of pushing one's boundaries past chilly to cold may have psychological implications in terms of developing resilience and faith in one's abilities. It all sounds good on paper, but despite all the scientific studies, many of us would rather take a walk in the cold than a dip in ice water!

According to a study published in the *American Journal of Human Biology*, we burn 34 percent more calories when we hike in cold weather than in more clement conditions. It makes intuitive sense—the physical exertion of tromping through snow or navigating ice is combined with the energy it takes to stay warm. And walking in cold air is by its nature invigorating and energizing, which means (if we do not get too cold) we are able to sustain a brisk pace for longer than we can on a hot summer's day.

IN STEP WITH NATURE

Even (or perhaps especially) when it is cold outside, go for a walk! And try to do it when the sun is shining brightest. Not only is this likely be the easiest time of day for a trek, but you will benefit from a dose of vitamin D. Among its many benefits, this "sunshine vitamin" can strengthen the immune system and boost your mood, which so many of us become deficient in during the winter. Of course, where you walk matters. If you live in a climate like Boston, Massachusetts, in the US, you will need to spend 23 minutes outside at noon to produce enough vitamin D for the day.

Mindfulness practice

The Discourse on the Foundations of Mindfulness is a core Buddhist meditation practice that is said to cultivate awareness and compassion. The foundations comprise four parts:

• Mindfulness of Body: paying attention to physical sensations, without getting caught up in analyses or judgment.

• Mindfulness of Feelings: paying attention to all our feelings—whether unpleasant, neutral, or pleasant—by allowing instead of pushing away.

• Mindfulness of the Mind: paying attention to our thoughts and emotions, simply noticing them without suppressing or obsessing.

• Mindfulness of Dhammas: also known as the nature of reality or the way things are. This involves paying attention to the phenomenal world (the world as it appears, and is understood by, humans). As with body, feelings, and mind, we notice, acknowledge, and—like watching clouds in a winter sky—let our observations drift away.

Now, take this ancient practice, which can be adapted to any belief system, and apply it to walking in the cold.

• The first part is quite easy—pay attention to the cold on your skin, from your forehead to your toes. Where do you end and the weather begin? Where is the edge?

• As you walk, examine your feelings. Do you want to get this over with? Are you easing into it? Does it make you feel good?

• What is going on in your mind? By becoming mindful of your body and feelings, have you given more space to thoughts and emotions? Examine them and, like ice melting, let them glide away.

• Once you are in a space where your feelings and mind are opened and clear, what happens? Do you feel more connected to the world around you? More able to be present? To just ... be?

Breathe better

It seems pretty obvious to say that we need to breathe in order to live, but did you know you can use your breath to maximize your life span, combat stress, and manipulate the energetic flow in your body? Winter is an excellent time to focus on how to improve your breath, to combat low energy during the cold months and give more life to your mind, body, and spirit.

The Sanskrit word prana means both "life-force energy" and "breath;" it doesn't have a single direct translation or function. Prana is the root source of all the energy in the universe. All forces of nature are manifestations of prana. Think about your breath as a subtle force that not only fills your physical body with life-giving energetic oxygen, but also fills your mind and emotional body with energetic vitality. When we inhale deeply and consciously, we are breathing oxygen into our lungs as well as taking in the environment and knowledge found in all of life.

Prana is the driving force behind all things. It is prana that keeps things moving in and around us. Without prana, life is gray, dark, cloudy, and full of stagnant energy. With prana, life is bright, creative, open, full, loving, and flowing. Prana can be found in the food we eat, the liquid we drink, the air we breathe, the warmth of the sun, and the people and places around us. This is why relationships feel so good—we are transferring this pranic energy from person to person.

Ayurveda—a 5,000-year-old Indian medicinal system which focuses not only on the body, but also the mind and lifestyle of an individual—teaches that illness and symptoms of sickness are clear manifestations of obstructed or decreased pranic flow. If you aren't sure of how to begin healing yourself or practicing self-care, a good place to start is by practicing conscious breathing. What does it mean to be conscious of your breath? It means that you are aware of your own inhale/exhale and you can feel the energy of the air flowing in and out of your body. So, are you getting all of the prana you deserve? Answer the following questions as honestly as possible:

• Am I using my breath wisely?

• Am I gaining energy from the air I breathe, the food I eat, and the relationships I have?

• Do I utilize my full lung capacity?

• Am I aware of my surroundings?

• Do I gain strength from my breath?

• Do I deplete my energy with activities or people?

• Am I draining the energy of other people with my own energy?

• Is my life stressful and chaotic?

• Am I able to redirect negative energy into positive feelings?

• Is it hard for me to focus?

• Do I waste a lot of time and procrastinate daily?

• Are my thoughts, actions, and words overly self-critical and negative?

These questions are intended to help you see where you are on your journey, what areas you can improve upon, and where any imbalances may lie.

Breathing exercise to increase prana and release stress

This exercise is called a pranic breath. Start with one pranic breath and work your way up (in your own time) to ten. Do this practice at least once a day.

• Sit comfortably, cross-legged on the floor, if possible. You can use a bolster or blankets to prop your legs up or lean against a wall to help you sit up tall. Try to relax your shoulders, allowing your shoulder blades to roll down your back toward your waist. This will help to lift your chest up and create space for your rib cage to move freely.

• Place your palms together in front of your heart. Push with pressure against both palms to create an activation of energy between both spheres of the body.

• Gently close your lips and focus only on breathing through your nose.

• Inhale for the count of ten, breathing in deeply though your nose and drawing your breath down into your lungs. Feel the breath expanding in your rib cage and trickling down into your belly, expanding deeper and wider. Imagine this breath as a golden white light that is pulling in all of Mother Nature's beautiful invigorating energy and sucking it deep into your body.

• Once your lungs and belly are full of this life-giving air, hold your breath for the count of ten (or as long as possible). Focus all of this energy to your third eye (the middle point in between your eyebrows). Imagine this space filling with all the golden white light that is building and swirling with prana.

• Exhale for the count of ten. As you slowly exhale, imagine the golden white light showering over your whole body and leaving you energized and with all your senses vital.

Conscious eating

Eating should be approached as a sacred and sensual experience. It's especially important to be mindful and conscious of your eating during winter, when many of us can comfort eat to cope with low mood or overeat during the festive period. Here is a simple yet effective ritual to increase your connection to your food.

1 Before you eat, feel and sense what your body needs and is truly craving. Make decisions about the food you are going to eat based on what is best for your body in that moment and what will serve you long term.

2 Once you have prepared your meal, sit in a calm and quiet environment, draw your attention to the food on your plate, and say a prayer, mantra, or blessing over your food. Try to remove any negative energy that has been placed on your food, and be thankful that you have the means to nourish your being, body, mind, and spirit with this food. One of the main reasons why we say a blessing and infuse our food with positive energy is to help us remember that our food is energy. Food is fuel to nourish our bodies and it's important to honor that.

3 As you eat, slowly breath in through your nose and out through your nose. Deep breathing will help you slow down and feel your food. Not only will you taste your food with heightened senses, but also you will gain more energy.

4 Use the tools already embedded deep within your body. Chew your food as well as possible. The saliva in your mouth is loaded with digestive enzymes to help you break down your food before you even swallow it.

5 After you've eaten, draw attention to how each part of your body feels:

• Is the food giving you energy and love?

• Is your mind being nurtured?

• Do you feel you are absorbing all the nutrients?

• Do you feel happy?

Practice this ritual as often as you can. Choosing to be in a calm environment while you eat is choosing to heal your body through the practice of mindful eating. Try to abstain from negative conversation while you are dining with others—this will help your body stay in a calm and neutral state.

Energizing teas

All excellent alternatives to coffee, these health-giving recipes will boost your energy and vitality during the long winter months.

Ginger and jasmine infusion for energy

Try this restorative elixir anytime your energy level is low to bolster mind, body, and spirit.

1 teaspoon sliced fresh ginger root

1 teaspoon jasmine tea leaves

1 teaspoon peppermint tea leaves

2 cups (480ml) hot water

Place the ginger, jasmine, and peppermint in a pan and add the hot water. Let brew for 5 minutes, then strain and pour into a mug.

Chicory root cheer

If you love coffee, you might find that it also keeps you awake into the night and then, in order to function well in the morning, you have to get back on the coffee grind to keep going. Chicory has a similarly wonderful flavor to coffee, but it is caffeine-free and easier on the system. It is a commonly found bright blue wildflower, a member of the daisy family, but it is the parsnip-like roots that are what we use for roasting and grinding. You can find chicory roots at any natural grocery and might become such a fan that you will take a long break from coffee.

bunch of fresh organic chicory

sharp knife

roasting pan

clean, dry cloth

coffee grinder

coffee maker

mug

milk and/or sugar, to taste

Preheat the oven to 325°F/170°C/Gas 3. Rinse the chicory roots well in cool water. Cut them into small cubes and let dry on the cloth. Once the roots are dry, place them on the roasting pan and heat for a half hour. Toward the end of the cooking time, you should smell a delightful coffee-like scent. Take out the roasted roots and let them cool. Grind the root pieces like you would coffee beans and brew. Try your first cup of chicory coffee plain, so you taste the true earthy flavor of the root. In addition to giving your body a break from the stress of caffeine, chicory is very good for detoxing and is less well known for its magical properties of strength, good luck, frugality, and the removal of obstacles and curses.

Brain and body booster

We all need a pick-me-up once in a while, especially by the end of the week when our physical and emotion tank might be empty. Nettle leaves are full of iron and potassium, and drinking nettle tea is also said to help regulate blood sugar levels. This wild and spicy brew will soon have you moving and grooving again!

teakettle

1 quart (1 liter) freshly drawn water

2 teaspoons fresh nettle

½ teaspoon ginkgo

1 teaspoon fresh or dried licorice

1 teaspoon chopped cinnamon stick

1 teaspoon finely diced ginger root

mortar and pestle

1-quart (1-liter) sealable jar, such as a Mason jar

While you are boiling the water in the kettle, place the herbs into your mortar and grind them together until well mixed. Transfer the ground herbs to the jar and pour in the boiling water. Steep for a half hour, then strain. The yield should be enough for three big glasses. I suggest you drink one glass while still warm and store and refrigerate the rest in the jar.

The recommended dose per day is three glasses: in the morning, at lunchtime, and after dinner, twice a week. If you are feeling really run down, drink it every other day and you'll pep up quite soon!

Setting rituals and goals

Creating routine

The winter is a great time to put a strong daily routine into practice, as it can help you to cope with the weather and lack of sunlight, sleep better, and promote self-healing. To begin with, forming new routines can be challenging, so it's a good idea to write out your routine and tape it to the refrigerator or a bathroom mirror so you can be reminded regularly of the things that will help you find balance.

The best routines are those that are customized to an individual's way of life and particular needs. Take the morning and evening routine suggestions on the following pages and apply them to your own life in a mindful way.

If you forget to incorporate some of the tools on certain days, that's okay. Don't stress, these routines are there to help guide you toward a life full of wellness, not stress you out. Remember, this is a lifelong journey and these tools will always be available to you—this is not a temporary fix, this is a lifestyle shift.

Morning routine: the best start to your day

Sleeping and rising early

The way we begin our days sets the tone for our energy, determining how we will feel throughout the day and how well we sleep. Going to sleep early and rising early keeps our bodies on a natural cycle that helps them function at 100 percent. It's best to wake up before 6 a.m., though in the winter, when the sun rises much later, it is okay to rise before 7 a.m. Unless you are a morning person, rising early may be a challenge for you. During the first couple of weeks, you may feel that switching your sleep schedule around is counterintuitive, but once you begin to rise early, you'll see all the ways your body and mind optimize energy throughout the day.

Give thanks and say an internal prayer upon waking up—every new day is a blessing. Make your bed when you wake up, too.

Five-minute meditation

Early-morning meditation activates the bioelectric energy that helps to stimulate and direct energy to the pineal gland. The pineal gland is a pear-shaped gland in the

brain that regulates hormone functions, specifically melatonin, which regulates our sleep-wake cycles. When we meditate in the morning, we are activating this system so that it can send more energy to our brains. This is especially helpful during winter, when our natural sleep-wake cycles can be disrupted as there are fewer hours of sunlight (see page 26).

The act of meditation can help with focus, anxiety, mood disorders, energy levels, and overall mind–body balance. To meditate, sit in silence, focus on your breath, acknowledge any thoughts that come into your mind and let them pass.

Without force, eliminate

Our bodies accumulate a lot of toxins and waste while we sleep, which is why it's important to expel waste first thing in the morning. Pooping helps to cleanse the system and relieves stress from our organs.

Regular elimination is a really important function for our health. When we hold in or restrict the flow of elimination, it causes major stress on our bodies and organs. How you poop can tell you a lot about your constitution and health as well. Most people don't talk

about their poop, so many people don't even know if their poop is healthy. The better you know your body, the more you can help yourself heal.

If you are prone to constipation, a morning belly massage will aid in elimination. Use the tips of your index fingers to massage the small intestines in clockwise circular motions around the navel. Repeat a rotation of these circles three to five times. Do this massage while sitting on the toilet.

Wash your face

Wash your face with cool water and then gently wash your eyes with cool water as well. (Heat can build up in the eyes and cause irritation, so washing your eyes will help to keep them clear and calm.)

Washing your face and eyes with cool water upon waking up reduces inflammation and redness and invigorates the senses. This is one of the simplest acts of kindness you can do for yourself in the morning (especially if you're not a morning person). It's not actually necessary to wash your face with skincare products in the morning unless you experience night sweats and feel that your skin is extra oily. You don't want to strip your skin of its natural oil.

Brush your teeth and scrape your tongue

Once you add this activity to your morning routine, you won't want to go a day without it. Scraping the tongue gets the body ready to digest and taste food. It also removes any toxins that have accumulated in the body overnight. It's important to remove these toxins as they may prevent the digestive system from functioning optimally.

To scrape your tongue, hold a U-shaped stainless-steel or copper tongue scraper at both long ends, place the scraper toward the back of your tongue, taking care not to hit your teeth or go too far back to your tonsils. Using mild pressure, place the edge of the scraper on the back of your tongue and scrape toward the tip of your tongue in one fluid motion. Repeat this about five times, unless you feel that it hurts, which is a sign you have already removed toxins.

Always use a proper tongue-scraping tool; using something else, such as a spoon, could risk cutting the edge or middle of the tongue.

Drink warm water with fresh lemon juice

Drink 1½–3¾ cups (350–900 ml) warm water with fresh lemon juice (see page 78) in the morning. This will cleanse your bowels, promote digestion, and remove toxins. If you are not used to drinking water first thing in the morning, start with just 1 cup (250 ml), then build up to more when your body is used to it. It's best to consume warm water throughout the day—this aids in detoxification, helps maintain a healthy weight, and keeps skin clear.

Get moving

Start your day with movement, such as yoga, Pilates, or cycling. Movement doesn't have to be intense—it can be as simple as stretching or taking a short winter walk (see page 106). Movement helps keep circulation and blood flow healthy. Without movement, the body becomes stagnant. Moving first thing in the morning will wake up your body and give you more energy throughout the day.

Dry-brush your body

Dry-brushing your skin will kick-start your lymphatic system, which aids in detoxification. Dry-brushing also keeps skin soft, removes dry or dead skin, and helps to maintain healthy circulation.

To dry-brush your body, you will need a soft-bristle skin brush. Starting at your feet and using upward brush strokes, work your way up your body toward your heart. Dry-brush your entire body, excluding your face.

Take a warm shower or bath infused with essential oils

Most people don't have time to take a morning bath, but it's a beautiful way to start your day and set a positive energetic mood. Adding a couple of essential oils to your bathtub or shower in the morning will wake up your senses and invigorate your body. Essential oils such as citrus aid in boosting mood and focus.

Massage your face

After your shower, massage your face with a nourishing face oil, such as the Glowing Goddess Face Oil (see page 99), to protect and hydrate your skin. Rub the oil into your hands and then apply generously to your entire face and décolletage area. Using upward strokes, pay particular attention to puffy areas by pressing and releasing along the inflamed regions. Very gently massage around the eye area as well, moving the soft tissue and skin in an upward motion and taking care not to get oil in your eyes.

Drink celery juice elixir

Drinking Celery Juice Elixir (see page 59) before eating food in the morning may help improve your overall health. Celery juice is nature's electrolyte. Celery is rich in sodium, magnesium, potassium, chloride, and phosphorus, all of which help to restore the body's natural electrolyte balance. Celery also balances and alkalizes the body, improves digestion, reduces inflammation, restores adrenals, improves skin, reduces water retention, and lowers bad cholesterol levels.

Enjoy a healthy breakfast

It is important to eat a healthy breakfast before you start to work, teach, learn, or play. Food is our first form of medicine. Nourishing your body with foods that are balancing to your body is important in the process of self-healing. Without food, we have no fuel to burn.

Evening routine: preparing for restful sleep

Sleep nourishes your body like a mother nurtures her baby. It gives you everything: strength, fertility, knowledge, contentment, happiness, and life itself. Healthy physiological, psychological, and neurological functioning all depend on you getting enough quality sleep.

We all know that sleep is a basic human need, like eating and drinking, and yet many of us still believe that we can get by on less sleep with no negative consequences. In fact, obtaining a sufficient amount of quality sleep that's in sync with your body's natural internal clock is vital for your mental and physical health. Inadequate sleep is linked to a number of conditions, including heart disease, kidney disease, high blood pressure, diabetes, stroke, obesity, and depression.

So what's the secret to waking up happier and well-rested? It's a smarter nighttime routine. What we choose to do with our evening hours directly impacts our quality of sleep, significantly influencing our mood and energy levels the next day. The truth is, most of us spend our nights binge-watching TV shows, texting, and late-night snacking—none of which are great for catching quality sleep. The good news: revamping your bedtime routine can be easy—and fun.

Cultivating a soothing sleep routine will help you achieve the best sleep you'll ever have. As a starting point, create a clean sleeping space, invest in comfortable bedding and keep it simple: keep the bedroom temperature low, and use nightlights if you have to get up for the bathroom during the night. Organizing your bedroom to create an at-home sleeping sanctuary is key for keeping your mind relaxed and free of stimulation in the evening hours. Try to keep your use of electronic devices to a minimum and stop using them 30 minutes before bed.

In terms of a routine, use the following practices daily to enhance your sleep, bring sacredness to your bedtime, and balance your body and mind.

Set the mood

Light candles and play relaxing music or sounds to help you ease into bedtime. Take caution, however, and make sure to blow out candles before you fall asleep. Diffusing essential oils also offer a great way to create a sacred sleeping environment.

Drink a warm sleep milk

Milk is the first thing we humans consume after birth. Drinking spiced milk is like nurturing yourself with maternal care before bed. Make drinking the sleep milk on page 46 an introduction to your routine, and drink it as you follow the next steps.

Give yourself a massage

When warm oil is absorbed into the skin, it nourishes all parts of the body, enhances circulation, and stimulates the lymphatic system. The act of self-massage (see page 72) is a nurturing ritual involving the sense of touch. Oiling the external body helps to ground energy and relieve stress, which is helpful for winding down to sleep.

Give yourself a face mask

Paying attention to your head is a wonderful way to relax tight nerves and remove the stress of a long day. Make and apply the natural face mask from page 98 and let the herbal infusion intoxicate and calm your senses.

Write in your journal

Sometimes our minds take control of our senses and we can't rest because our mind isn't at rest. Journaling is a practice that can help soothe your thoughts and allow your mind to rest with ease. Keep a journal or notebook by your bedside and use it to write down your thoughts, whether it's a simple reminder, such as "don't forget to buy conditioner," a poem you're composing, or deep emotional feelings that need to be let out.

Give yourself a reflexology foot massage

Reflexology involves stimulating the reflex points on your feet, hands, face, or ears to subtly impact the entire body, affecting the organs and glands. It can transport you into a state of deep relaxation where you are open to suggestions you give yourself. There are nearly 15,000 nerves in your feet alone, which is one of many reasons why foot reflexology is so calming, soothing, and effective. A simple foot-massage routine just before you go to bed can help you drift off to sleep naturally. Use an massage oil such as Brahmi oil to help promote relaxation to the nerves and prevent insomnia.

To give yourself a foot massage, put 1 teaspoon of oil into the palm of your hand, rub your hands together and then massage the oil all over your feet. (If the skin of your feet is very dry, you may want to use more oil.) Using firm pressure, slowly massage along the arch of each foot. Massage back and forth along each foot, paying particular attention to any areas that feel sore. Do this massage for at least 10 minutes.

Take a relaxing bath

Taking time to bathe in the healing power of water can be transformative, and the perfect medicine for relaxing the body and mind after a hard day. The sensuous comfort water provides connects us back to both our bodies and the Earth's beauty. Try one of the bath recipes from pages 60, 90–91, 93, and 96.

Affirmations to focus on your goals

Many of us can fall into negative thought patterns during the winter, so it's an important time to focus on gently shifting your mindset to be more positive. The new year and the change of seasons from winter to spring are also natural times for renewal and setting new resolutions and goals, and positive thinking can help you to achieve them.

Positive thinking may not solve all of your problems, but negative thinking can greatly affect your outlook and reaction to life. The more you speak to yourself with negativity, the more you will suffer. Being negative is setting yourself up for failure, whereas being positive gives you an alternative route to finding happiness and peace. If you think positively, you will radiate and spread that upward energy to all areas of your life. Have you ever met someone who exudes happy energy and whose happiness just pours from their being effortlessly? If you have, that person most likely practices (on some level) shifting their energy to be more positive.

"If you think positively, you will radiate and spread that upward energy to all areas of your life."

The way we think and talk to ourselves also directly affects our health. We always have a choice in life, to succumb to our woes or find new ways to overcome them. If you choose the latter, you will see the difference in your life, health, and overall happiness. However, it is important to find time to revel in your thoughts and emotions and to acknowledge your feelings and not suppress them. When we hold in our emotions, we are actually dulling our vibration and manifesting dis-ease.

Affirmations are a statement or phrase that we repeat regularly to set our intention and bring about change. They can help us stay focused on our goals. If you repeat an affirmation on a daily basis you are engraining the essence of those words inside your subconscious mind, which will help you remain positive in times of distress. You could tape this affirmation to your bathroom mirror and repeat it over and over again while you're doing your morning routine until you're finished.

Affirmation exercise

When your headspace feels crowded with unnecessary thoughts and your energy is low, it's time for a pick-me-up. This is a quick exercise to relieve stress, discard unwanted negative energy, and bring focus to the present moment. You can practice this anywhere, at any time. It's not necessary to sit in a meditative state but this will help in the process of shifting your thoughts and energy.

• Find a space that is safe and sacred to you and make it as comfortable as possible. Sit with your eyes open or closed.

• Breathe deeply, inhaling and exhaling through your nose for the count of five. Allow the air to fill your stomach and expand your rib cage and imagine it traveling all the way up to the top of your crown. With each inhale, visualize your breath creating a golden bubble around your body.

• Say this affirmation.

"My intention is to be at peace with myself; eliminate toxic feelings, elements, and energies from my life; unlearn negative and harmful practices and thought patterns; stop checking for people who don't check for me; create space for myself that is nurturing for my personal growth so that I may generate loving energy for myself and for others; nourish my spirit; and balance my energies. I have big dreams and I deserve to live a life I love and let that love radiate, today and every day I grace the Earth with my presence."

Resources

Essential oils

The quality of essential oils you use is important. They should always be organic and without fillers. If you are buying generic essential oils cheaply, look into the sourcing of the brand to make sure they meet the standards of a good-quality oil.

Young Living (youngliving.com/en_US and youngliving.com/en_GB—UK) has set the bar high for the way essential oils should be made with its own seed-seal process. These quality commitments are built upon three pillars: sourcing, science, and standards. Young Living carries an array of essential oils, household cleaning solutions, supplements, and body-care and baby products.

For advice on using essential oils safely, go to www.aromaweb.com/articles/safety.asp

Spices and herbs

Always choose organic and minimally processed spices and herbs. Buying herbs in bulk can be beneficial in the long run. Below are some suggested suppliers, but you can also source many organic herbs in bulk from Amazon, Whole Foods, or your local boutique natural medicine stores.

Mountain Rose Herbs

mountainroseherbs.com (US/Canada only) has a wide selection of bulk herbs, spices, loose-leaf teas, essential oils, and herbal extracts. You can find organic options on the website.

Banyan Botanicals

banyanbotanicals.com (US only) is another option for herbs and spices, including triphala (as well as essential oils). Its products are organic.

Maharishi Ayurveda

mapi.com and maharishi.co.uk carry Ayurvedic herbs (such as triphala), high-quality massage oils, and lifestyle supplements.

The journal of the American Botanical Council

abc.herbalgram.org includes a database of herbs and their uses.

botanical.com is a great online herbal encyclopedia.

Sun Potion

sunpotion.com is an international supplier of herbs and adaptogens, including triphala (see page 76).

Dandelion Botanical Company

dandelionbotanical.com is a U.S. natural apothecary supplying certified organic herbs, spices, and botanicals.

The Edible Flower Company

theedibleflowergarden.co.uk carry a huge variety of organic edible flowers grown in Devon, England, UK.

Magnesium flakes

Omica Organics (omicaorganics.com) carries the most potent magnesium flakes you'll find on the market.

Epsom salts

SaltWorks (seasalt.com—US only) carries organic Epsom salts in bulk. If you are planning on taking plenty of baths, you could purchase the 50 lb (22.6kg) bag. You can also find Epsom salts at your local pharmacy and health food store.

Raw honey

Beekeeper's Naturals

beekeepersnaturals.com practice sustainable beekeeping and are a trusted source for raw honey. None of their bee pollen or honey is ever heated or treated with chemicals or preservatives.

Accessories

It's not necessary to buy all these products at once, but if you feel in alignment with any of them in particular, try incorporating them into your routines and rituals.

Tongue scrapers (see page 123)

You can order a stainless steel or copper tongue scraper on Amazon or find one at a health food store.

Skin brushes (see page 124)

Karmameju (capbeauty.com/collections/karmameju—US only) carries body and facial brushes.

Candles

The type of candle you buy is important because you want the air in your home to be as clean as possible. Choose candles made from nontoxic, organic coconut wax, beeswax, or soy wax. They will infuse your home with beautiful scents.

Making your own skincare products

(see pages 94–99)

The suppliers listed below sell a range of natural oils, fats, and waxes to make your own products. Do shop around as some sell ingredients that the others may not and prices do vary.

UK

Fresholi

www.fresholi.co.uk sells essential oils, butters, and waxes.

The Soap Kitchen

www.thesoapkitchen.co.uk sells good value basics such as bicarbonate of soda as well as a range of oils and butters.

www.naturallythinking.co.uk

Aromatherapy supplies as well as jars and bottles.

www.gracefruit.com

Oils, waxes, and butters plus lip balm tins.

www.nealsyardremedies.com

Good-quality essential oils and herbs.

www.aqua-oleum.co.uk

Good-quality essential oils and aromatherapy supplies (owned by Julia Lawless).

www.baldwins.co.uk

Dried herbs and herbal tinctures.

USA

These suppliers sell an extensive range of oils and waxes.

www.teachsoap.com

www.brambleberry.com

www.makingcosmetics.com

www.theherbarie.com

www.lotioncrafter.com

www.wholesalesuppliesplus.com

Index

Credits

Text credits

© **Caroline Artiss:** page 97

© **Christine Burke:** pages 40–41, 62–63, 68–69, 74–75, 84–85, and 100–101

© **Elisabeth Carlsson:** pages 34–37 and 57

© **Cerridwen Greenleaf:** pages 22–23, 30, 33, 42–43, 44–45, 49, 50–51, 52–53, 54, 59, 60, 66–67 (Wellbeing ritual), 90, 93 (Moisturizing coconut bath), 94, 96, 98, and 116–118

© **Noelle Renée Kovary:** pages 46 (Sleep milk), 70–73, 76, 78–80, 82–83, 91 (Detox bath), 93 (Rose milk bath), 99, 104–106, 110–113, 114, and 120–134

© **Lottie Muir:** pages 54 (The healing power of honey) and 81

© **Alice Peck:** pages 10–20, 24–29, 87–88, and 107–108

© **Silja Sample:** pages 46 (Sweet dreams tea), 55, and 56

Image credits

Debi Treloar: pages 18, 35, 36, 37, 45, 47, 55, 67, 108, 122, 126, 129, and 130; **Francesca Yorke:** page 22; **Emma Mitchell:** page 24; **Catherine Gratwicke:** page 31; **Georgia Glynn-Smith:** page 32; **Belle Daughtry:** page 43; **Erin Kunkel:** page 48; **Lisa Linder:** page 51; **Kate Whitaker:** page 54; **Kim Lightbody:** page 56; **Yuki Sugiura:** page 58; **William Reavell:** pages 59 and 81; **Earl Carter:** page 61; **Stuart West:** pages 71, 95, and 96; **Polly Wreford:** page 72; **Geoff Dann:** page 73; **Peter Cassidy:** page 78; **Paul Ryan:** page 89; **Winfried Heinze:** pages 91 and 99; **Anastasiia Krivenok:** page 92; **Toby Scott:** page 115; **Helen Cathcart:** page 116; **Lucinda Symons:** page 119; **Jaroslaw Grudzinski:** page 121; **Clare Winfield:** page 125 below

Adobestock.com: Sara: pages 8–9, **nataba:** pages 10–11; **DariaS:** page 13; **vectorwin:** page 14; **Maria Raz:** pages 16–17; **Teppi:** page 17; **Lightfield Studios:** page 21; **psynovec:** page 27; **stone36:** page 29; **dachux21:** pages 38–39; **Maryna:** page 41; **yanikap:** page 53; **HN Works:** page 63; **yganko:** pages 64–65; **Oli:** page 69; **fizkes:** page 75; **alexugalek:** page 77; **igorp17:** page 79; **Esin Deniz:** page 80; **scabrn:** page 85; **Cavan Images:** page 86; **kidza:** page 90; **Ann Stryzhekin:** page 101; **maxa0109:** pages 102–103; **ahavelaar:** page 105; **Jag_cz:** page 111; **nilanka:** page 112; **Marcus Z-pics:** page 125 above; **Christian:** page 132–133; **Ricardo:** page 135; **vegefox.com:** snowflake pattern on pages 17, 23, 25, 27, 49, 51, 54, 56, 68, 80, 83, 90–91, 98, 107, and 134